Praise for *Lov*

What a brilliant resource for anyone wl ....inking of joining the wider teaching profession as a tutor. Packed with encouragement, wisdom, practical advice and stories from tutors, this is a fantastic resource. Highly recommended!

**Professor Dame Alison Peacock, CEO,
Chartered College of Teaching**

This is a really important and useful book for those who already tutor, those who are thinking about it, and those who are wondering where all the classroom teachers went. Julia offers a very thoughtful and, at times, personal account of what it is to be a tutor, and how important the role is in shaping children's lives. It's also a very useful text for those curious about tutoring as a career path. Tutoring isn't just an 'add-on', it's a Sherpa-style approach to teaching and learning, and, for us readers, Julia is a fantastic guide.

Hywel Roberts, teacher, writer and speaker

Love Tutoring is an important book: it locates the role of tutoring in its historical and current context. It's an element of provision that we all ought to know more about. Julia Silver is an expert in the field; she also has a gift for communicating complex ideas, and I certainly feel better informed and more appreciative of tutoring as a result of reading this terrific book.

Mary Myatt, education writer and speaker

Julia's passion for tutors and tutoring shines through in her beautifully thought-out handbook for thoughtful tutoring. She sets out big ideas and translates these into practical pause points and reflective moments which make the book informed, engaging, readable and practical. Superb.

Dr Fiona Aubrey-Smith, Director of One Life Learning

Love Tutoring is a beacon of insight for both novice and experienced tutors alike. Authored by enthusiastic, experienced and passionate Julia Silver, this book is a treasure trove of practical wisdom, offering invaluable guidance on every aspect of the tutoring profession.

It challenges the prevailing narratives surrounding tutoring, advocating for its recognition as a vital and respected profession in the field of education. Drawing on her extensive experience as both a tutor and a teacher, Julia Silver eloquently argues for a paradigm shift in how tutoring is perceived and valued by society.

Sue Atkins, parenting broadcaster, speaker and author of
The Can-Do Kid's Journal: Discover Your Confidence Superpower!
www.thesueatkins.com

Julia Silver

LOVE TUTORING

Be the tutor your student needs

Crown House Publishing Limited
www.crownhouse.co.uk

First published by

Crown House Publishing Limited
Crown Buildings, Bancyfelin, Carmarthen, Wales, SA33 5ND, UK
www.crownhouse.co.uk

and

Crown House Publishing Company LLC
PO Box 2223, Williston, VT 05495, USA
www.crownhousepublishing.com

Cover image © Анастасия Норина – stock.adobe.com. Canary image: 28
studios., Phoenix image: SimpleLine, Dove image: Anastasiia – vecteezy.com.
Celebration station graphic © Adhi – stock.adobe.com.

First published 2024.

British Library Cataloguing-in-Publication Data

A catalogue entry for this book is available from the British Library.

Print ISBN 9781785836831
Mobi ISBN 9781785837227
ePub ISBN 9781785837234
ePDF ISBN 9781785837241

LCCN 2024933114

Printed and bound in the UK by
CPi, Antony Rowe, Chippenham, Wiltshire

To my father, Jonathan Samuel Stewart – wish you were here.

To my mother, Havi Stewart – my first tutor.

FOREWORD

From the moment I picked up this book, I was visited by a flood of memories: of my many past students and of myself as a callow and unsupported but ever hopeful tutor. I wish that Julia Silver's *Love Tutoring* had been available to me at the beginning of my career in education, but at least I can happily endorse – from my vantage point so many years on – the insights and wisdom it contains.

I was an accidental tutor. In my first year of university, I was asked by a friend to tutor his younger sister through her final year of English. She had friends who also needed tutoring. Then there were the younger siblings of other friends who asked for help. Soon, I was advertising in the local paper – remember the local paper? – which involved going into a very dusty and rather depressing office and paying a dollar per word in cash to advertise my expertise and availability in a tiny little box on the classifieds page.

Tutoring was a way to make a passable income whilst I was a full-time university student. I tutored in the evenings and all day on Saturdays from my bedroom in my family home – styled to look less like a bedroom and more like a study – and ushered young people up and down the stairs whilst my family looked on, highly amused.

I set and marked homework and supervised mock exams to get them prepared for the real thing. I talked to parents and gave a wide array of advice which I was certainly insufficiently experienced to give. I even took four of my students to the theatre for the very first time – a matinee performance of *A Midsummer Night's Dream* at the Sydney Opera House. It still shocks me that their private school had never organised an excursion to the theatre. Over 30 years later, I remember stealing quick looks at their faces as they sat next to me in the dark: bewildered, amused, awe-struck.

I had high expectations for my students (looking back, I was actually a rather brutal task master) but no expectations for myself. I considered it lucky that there were young people – who were, in truth, only slightly younger than me – who wanted to learn from me, and I was relieved that I appeared to have a positive impact on their learning and their results. But in my mind, what I did wasn't *real* teaching, and I wasn't a *real* educator. For me, tutoring was Plan B, as Julia Silver so evocatively puts it in this important and timely analysis of the role of the tutor.

Moreover, I had no idea how to measure my success beyond my students' exam results and anecdotal data, no community of practice to support and guide me, nothing in place to protect me as I went into the houses of strangers and welcomed strangers into my own home, and no sense of the value I was providing. I had none of the safety or support that Silver advocates for, and not much of the skill either. Perhaps it is no wonder that I did not take the role seriously and sought professional legitimacy elsewhere.

As I read *Love Tutoring*, I was struck anew by the absurd double-standard that applies to tutoring. In increasing numbers, parents and students seek the support of tutors at some point in their learning journey. As Silver outlines clearly in Chapter 2, there is a wealth of evidence for the effectiveness of tutoring, both one-to-one and in small groups. Indeed, in a number of countries it has become a key government strategy to boost academic results, support underperforming students and address educational disruption. Two examples of this are the UK's National Tutoring Programme (NTP) and the COVID Intensive Learning Support Program in New South Wales, Australia.

The tutoring model existed long before the classroom model (which was very much a product of the Industrial Revolution), and its success quite simply stands to reason. Any student will benefit from having the attention, experience and time of an expert educator. Even with my staggering inexperience at the age of 19, I had recent experience of exactly what my students were training for; time to spend listening to them and answering their questions; patience to help them practice (and a bit of youthful arrogance to inoculate me against doubt and insecurity). It is becoming increasingly clear that the traditional classroom does not fit all students, and that neurodiverse students and/or those with additional learning needs are particularly underserved and even alienated by the classroom model of education.

And yet, as Silver reminds us, tutors are 'underdeveloped, underrepresented and underestimated'. The negative view of tutoring comes from within as well as outside the education profession. I have worked with many teachers who bitterly resent any sign that their students are being tutored, even though they themselves tutor students from other schools. The reluctance to acknowledge the value and popularity of tutoring – indeed, the refusal to see tutors as education professionals at all – makes the position of the tutor precarious and lonely, and only serves to discourage parents and students from seeking the support that will make so much difference to students' lives. So, as Silver says, 'For tutoring to become a trusted part of the educational landscape, it needs to grow up.' This book shows us what the maturity of tutoring should look like.

Love Tutoring is a celebration of the privilege and joy that comes from working with young people as well as a description of the challenges that tutors and those who use their services face whilst they operate in silos and without the professional standards that would provide a structure for accountability and quality assurance. This book is part manifesto, part tutor workbook. As the founder of Qualified Tutor, a professional development organisation for the UK tutoring profession which is committed to raising standards and building a supportive and engaged community, it is appropriate that Silver has showcased the stories of individual members to demonstrate the diversity within the tutoring profession and the many ways in which tutors support their students. These stories are deeply powerful and even moving. Silver isn't only about inspiration, though. In this book, she takes tutors and potential tutors through the process of setting up a viable and safe business. Throughout the book, there are prompts to encourage self-reflection and she also, most generously, encourages her readers to contact her directly with their questions. This book is a manifestation of Silver's absolute commitment to the development of a sustainable professional pathway for tutors, to let tutors step out of the shadows and be recognised and held accountable for the important work they do.

Even whilst I continued to think of tutoring as my Plan B, I returned to it many times – as a post-graduate student in London, as an academic, and even whilst I was a full-time high school teacher and head of department. And then, out of the blue, tutoring officially moved from Plan B to Plan A. I joined a start-up team building an online tutoring platform which was to become Australia's largest online tutoring service, Cluey Learning. As the Chief Learning Officer at Cluey, I learned a huge amount about edtech, product development, PR, marketing, and business practices, but at the heart of everything Cluey built what I have learned as an educator – including as an accidental tutor – about the unique role and value of the tutor within the modern education ecosystem.

I urge all the many tutors and potential tutors to proceed with Julia Silver's insightful words as your guide and inspiration. As I am sure Julia would herself suggest: take the time on a regular basis to make a cup of tea, set out a plate of Petit Beurres (or Tim Tams for the Australian contingent) and work through these chapters so that you can reflect on your current, and aspirational, practice by bringing more clarity, structure, sense, inspiration and joy into students' lives.

Dr Selina Samuels has spent her entire life in education (since the age of 2-and-a-half) – either having it done to her or doing it to others. She has been a tutor, teacher, head of department and senior school leader, university lecturer, advisor to schools, and specialist in pedagogy and edtech. She was the founding Chief Learning Officer at Cluey Learning and is currently the Global Director of Teaching and Learning for a worldwide network of schools.

PREFACE

Those of us who struggle in the school environment, sensitive to a system that values compliance over creativity, are like the canaries that coal miners carried underground to detect toxic gases.

Those of us who get back up again after endless hurts, after breaking down or giving up, are like the mythological phoenix rising from the ashes to find a new way of being.

Those of us who take that learning and point it towards the next generation, determined to find a gentler and more effective approach are like the dove that points to a new world of possibility.

This book is written for the canaries, for the phoenixes and for the doves. May you soar.

ACKNOWLEDGEMENTS

It has taken me four years to write this book. Actually, that's not true. It took six months to write the book, and then another three-and-a-half years to let it go out into the world. These are the people who helped to make that happen:

David Bowman, Emma Tuck, Beverley Randell, Lucy Delbridge, my wonderful publishing team, who believed in this book before I did.

A. J. Harper and the Top Three community, who always put the reader first.

Seth Godin and Sir Ken Robinson, the teachers of my heart, who point towards better ways.

David Rones, my business mentor, who just gets it.

Odette Wohlman, my business partner, who has the biggest heart of anyone I have met.

Simon Silver, my rock and my best friend.

Michael, Benjamin, Rina, Daniel and Sara, my children and all-time favourite people.

And, of course, the Qualified Tutor members – this book is for you.

CONTENTS

The fact is that given the challenges we face, education doesn't need to be reformed – it needs to be transformed. The key to this transformation is not to standardize education, but to personalize it, to build achievement on discovering the individual talents of each child, to put students in an environment where they want to learn and where they can naturally discover their true passions.

Ken Robinson, *The Element: How Finding Your Passion Changes Everything*

Instead of wondering when your next vacation is, maybe you should set up a life you don't need to escape from.

Seth Godin, *Tribes: We Need You to Lead Us*

Part I

TUTORING IS NOT PLAN B

Chapter 1

SAFE, SKILLED AND SUPPORTED

Learning Can Be Lovely

I have a very specific tutoring niche. I love to work with primary-age students who need a more personalised approach – those gentle souls struggling in boisterous classrooms who crave an opportunity to learn in a calm and reassuring space.

Give me a timid 9-year-old suffering with maths anxiety, and I will give them the time and space to really explore and experiment with mathematical thinking.

Give me an under-stimulated 11-year-old, eager to go beyond the confines of the curriculum, and we will create an awesome research project together.

Give me a 7-year-old who has gaps in their learning from a curriculum that is too fast-paced and an environment that is too distracting, and we will slow right down and take as much time as necessary to build solid foundations.

I have tutored on and off since I was seventeen, but when, at 31, my third child was born, I decided to try to make a career of it. As a qualified teacher in a close-knit community, word spread quickly about my tutoring. Within two weeks, I had filled my schedule and, even more excitingly, I was hopeful that I could make a real difference to these young people.

At first it was delightful. Whilst my own children were sleeping or settled with a babysitter, the students came to my home, shuttled back and forth by eager parents. I would open the front door and warmly welcome the child in, waving their parents away with a confident smile.

Coming to me for tutoring was probably good fun. My home is an inviting and encouraging learning environment. On the bookcase, *The Gruffalo* and *Elmer* (the patchwork elephant) nestle amongst hundreds of much-loved and well-thumbed children's books. The cupboards are stacked with Numicon and Kinetic Sand, playing cards, dice and modelling clay. The walls are covered with posters, sticky notes and magic whiteboard paper. If we are counting, it will be with coloured pegs. If we are writing, it will be with scented gel pens. This is my way of setting out my stall, of creating a playful and welcoming environment that students can relax into and enjoy. It is my way of demonstrating that learning can be lovely, which is what my tutoring is all about. I use play-based, open-ended activities to bring back the natural love of learning that we all felt in our earliest years.

We usually sat across a corner of my kitchen table, the student at the head of the table and me on the mustard yellow bench against the wall. I always started with an enthusiastic, 'I'm so glad to see you!' or 'How's your day been so far?' I would give them a little time to chat, trying to really see and hear them, to connect with them and how they felt right there in the moment.

Then I would share my schedule for the session. I like to combine maths and English to keep things fresh and to build on strengths as well as weaknesses. For ease of planning and a sense of continuity, at least one of the activities tends to be a long-term project, such as a book we are reading together or a longer piece of writing.

About halfway through, I would stop to put some biscuits on a plate and pour a glass of juice for the student, who by then would be deeply engaged in an independent task. Sometimes I would put on some quiet instrumental music whilst they worked. For the final activity of the session, we would do something lighter – some maths games or comic poetry – as they nibbled on a Petit Beurre.

When they left, it would be calmly and with a smile. It was an enjoyable hour in a quiet home with a friendly and reassuring adult. If nothing else, I had provided a welcome respite from the crowded classroom.

In my imagination, tutoring was the perfect job. It was fulfilling and flexible. It enabled me to make a difference on my own terms. But, again and again, at precisely the same point, I would begin to come unstuck.

The fifth session is usually when a tutor shifts gear into the long, slow work of making progress. By now, we have had the time to really assess the student and build up a rapport. We have found out what they know and can do, and how they feel about learning. We may also have picked up some quick wins along the way, such as reading the clock or multiplying fractions.

But learning is a marathon, not a sprint, and progress is not linear. It is a messy and organic process. Tutoring, especially for primary-age students, means revisiting the same skills in myriad different ways. They need to revise and apply what they are learning repeatedly, practising until they are confident. Switching activities before they tire and coming up with yet another way of approaching the same concept takes time and bucket loads of persistence.

But a month in, and the novelty begins to wear off. The parents begin to get antsy. Hope has been replaced with impatience. They are wondering: has it helped? Have we done enough? How long can we afford to continue?

Or, maybe, to be totally honest, it is not the parents getting antsy. Maybe it is me. Maybe it is not the parents doubting me. Maybe I am doubting myself, my ability to be the tutor my student needs.

I struggled on, but my smile became strained. Within a few months tutoring began to feel like a burden, not a blessing. It became the field for an internal battle, a clash of my values and beliefs. I felt alone, bored and insecure. This wasn't the no-brainer career I had expected when I started out.

The Plan B Mindset

Is there a professional working within the education sector who is as misunderstood as the tutor? Teaching assistants, speech and language therapists, and peripatetic music teachers are all absorbed into the generally well-intentioned, gently forward-moving juggernaut of the mainstream school system. But, with only a few exceptions, tutors have been left out in the cold. We contribute in the background, boosting results and rehabilitating learners, but we are rarely given a seat at the table.

This cycle of neglect, fuelled by a lack of representation in mainstream education, led one influential paper to call private tuition 'shadow schooling' and 'the hidden secret of education'.[1] These phrases are deeply problematic. Those of us who already love tutoring take our role and responsibilities very seriously. We recognise that our greatest impact is on the confidence, resilience and self-esteem of our students. Helping a young person to gain a passing grade in functional maths or to discover a love of biology goes well beyond academic results. It gives purpose, meaning and hope to the student and their tutor.

Mainstream education has turned its back on tutoring for too long. Leaving tutors to languish in the shadows is irresponsible. It makes it harder to keep children safe, and it means that tutors aren't receiving the support and development that every professional needs to do their best work.

Too often, I read posts about tutoring as a great 'side hustle'. In the United States, the phrase simply means a second job, but to my British ears, 'hustling' evokes cowboys, pirates and smarmy second-hand car-dealers. No wonder many tutors wince when they tell people what they do for a living.

Tutoring is not yet seen as a first-choice career. Every tutor I know came to it in their own way and for their own reasons. Many of us

---

1   Peter Lampl, Foreword. In P. Kirby, *Shadow Schooling: Private Tuition and Social Mobility in the UK* (London: Sutton Trust, 2016), p. 1. Available at: https://www.suttontrust.com/our-research/shadowschooling-private-tuition-social-mobility.

left the classroom or the corporate world for a life less rigid. Some of us tutor when we retire or whilst we study or apply for graduate positions. A few of us have long-term health issues or are caring for someone else. In fact, in the hundreds of interviews I have conducted with tutors, I have never yet met anyone who intended to become a tutor. Instead, I hear 'I couldn't afford childcare, so I became a tutor.' 'My managers weren't understanding of my chronic health issues, so I decided to tutor.' 'I needed to pay off my student debt, so I thought I'd tutor.' 'I couldn't face another minute in the classroom, so I figured I'd tutor.' This is what I call the 'Plan B mindset', and I believe it has a lot to answer for.

In my case, I chose not to go back to the classroom after I'd had children because it was too much to juggle. In 2009, I had three children under 5 years of age. Childcare would have cost more than my teacher's salary, and being at home with my kids felt right, but we needed a second income. Plus, the stamina required to teach thirty individuals full time was something I didn't think I could sustain – and still don't. I wouldn't have had the energy to come home and look after my own kids. I knew it was just too much. So I decided to tutor.

I now know that I am not alone in side-stepping a lifetime of classroom service. Many teachers have taken the same decision in recent years to guard their well-being, choosing to repurpose their skill sets as tutors rather than allowing themselves to be crushed under the weight of the school system.

I have interviewed tutors at **every level of expertise from all over the world**, and they all agree that **tutoring can be lonely**.

And it is not only teachers who are turning to tutoring as a career choice. I know of professionals from accounting to marketing, pharmaceuticals to social work, and even the police force, who have left their positions to explore a role in tutoring. But no matter what our path into tutoring looks like, the only way to be trusted and accepted by the wider teaching community is to approach our work with care and commitment and to ensure that we always put the needs of our students first.

That'll Do, Pig

Tutoring can be a solitary existence. More than a decade later, I can still feel the loneliness that would crash over me as I stood by the kitchen window anticipating the arrival of the next student. Yes, I was grateful to be able to stay at home with my children and still work, but I felt isolated. This feeling is not unique to me and my lived experience. I have interviewed tutors at every level of expertise from all over the world, and they all agree that tutoring can be lonely.

I do my best thinking when I talk over issues with peers and mentors – with people who 'get it'. In a primary school, there is usually a friendly teacher or wise teaching assistant happy to spend ten quiet minutes discussing your kids or your lessons. Just having someone with whom to share a cup of tea and a biscuit or exchange some words of encouragement can give you the courage and the confidence to keep going.

What I craved was professional dialogue. With no staffroom, no colleagues down the hall and no leader to lean on, I had no one with whom I could 'talk tutoring'. With no one to give me a nod or a thumbs up, the self-doubt became crippling. If you know the Dick King-Smith book *The Sheep-Pig* – or its delightful movie adaptation, *Babe* – you will remember the moment right at the end when the farmer looks down at Babe and says, in his gruff voice full of love and pride, 'That'll do, Pig.' At the end of a great tutoring session, *that* was the feeling I craved: a pat on the head or a nod of approval. But none came.

I am not proud of this feeling. I don't believe that the approval of others is the correct measure of my worth, but I was accustomed to positive feedback and I felt lost without it. This goes right to the heart of our modern education system, which uses reward and punishment for crowd control and micro-management. We have been trained to respond to our master's voice ('Good girl', 'Great job') and to praise and certificates. Then, as we grow older, promotions and bonuses become the currency by which we learn to measure our success.

In most sectors, the customer is always right. Happy testimonials are the best way to evaluate a service. We receive verbal and non-verbal feedback from our students and clients; a groan or a cheer, a thank you or a cold shoulder; a referral or a rotten testimonial. But even though I received only great feedback, I felt terribly uncomfortable. Was I a good tutor or just a likeable tutor? Did my clients know the difference? Were they happy because they were making progress, or was it just the cookies and juice that made them smile? Surely, there was more to tutoring than keeping people happy? In professions like medicine, law and education, the client doesn't always have all the facts. When parents aren't educators and don't know their children as learners, are they the best arbiters of my practice?

What I needed in those early days was a solid idea of what 'good' looks like in tutoring. I needed a meaningful and objective way to measure my impact and understand how I needed to improve. I felt that I didn't know how to tutor, that I was making it up as I went along, extrapolating from the teaching and parenting skills I had developed in my other roles. That isn't to say that I was doing it wrong, I just didn't know whether I was doing it right. I also needed peers and mentors to help me stay on the right path and push through when I felt like giving up. I needed support and guidance. I needed a community of practice.

Looking back more than a decade to that young teacher tutoring from her kitchen table, what felt at the time like personal insecurity, I now recognise as professional integrity. I wanted to be the best tutor I could be. I wanted to feel a sense of progress, both for my students and for myself. I wanted to be proud of what I had achieved and excited to keep going.

Find Your Element as a Tutor and Fly

That feeling I craved, of loving tutoring, was what educationalist Sir Ken Robinson called being in your Element, with a capital 'E' (which is why I have capitalised the term in this book). In his extensive work on the subject, he told story after story of people who had struggled to walk a mainstream path and then soared once they had tapped into their innate abilities and aligned with the world around them. He said that 'finding your Element is essential to your well-being and ultimate success'.[2] Sir Ken said that when we find our Element we can achieve far more than we might imagine.

Tutoring can be flexible and fulfilling. As we will see in the following chapters, there are many more types of tutor than ever before. That is why I believe it is a space that lends itself to finding your Element. If you have a passion for maths, or reading, or young people with autism, you can build a niche for yourself.

In this book, I will show you how and why tutoring might be a brilliant path for you. I will show you many examples of people who found that they were able to develop their true talents through tutoring. These are individuals I know well and who are inspiring and authentic humans. Some work three hours a day whilst they raise their young families. Some have more than matched their teaching salary with online group tuition or international tutoring. Some have developed alternative provision to support disadvantaged young people or built tutoring franchises of every size and specialism. In every case, the common thread is that they each started out like you and me: intrigued by the promise of tutoring but not quite sure what was possible.

. . . .

2   K. Robinson and L. Aronica, *The Element: How Finding Your Passion Changes Everything* (New York: Penguin, 2009), p. 8.

The first thing to realise is that tutoring is incredibly adaptable. Not only does it allow you to personalise learning to the needs of the student, but it also allows you to personalise the way you work to suit your own needs. If you have mobility or health issues that require you to work from home and rest regularly, that is possible. If you want to travel the world whilst you tutor, or help ambitious but disadvantaged students get into top universities, or build a business you could one day sell for millions, all that is possible too. There are so many right ways to be a tutor, and I hope that by the time you finish reading this book, you will have found one that will work for you.

You might be thinking, but who are we, who were born and raised within systems that teach us to conform and comply, to have the guts and the gumption to find our Element and chart our own course? Actually, I think the real question is: who are we not to?

Our world has a greater need for thriving and successful people than ever. As G. Michael Hopf observes, 'Hard times create strong men, strong men create good times, good times create weak men, and weak men create hard times.' We are living in hard times right now, and we need strong people to make things good again.

We need to make things good for our young people, and we need to make things good for ourselves. This is not a time to put our own needs to one side. Rather, it is a time to wholeheartedly align our unique abilities with the needs of the next generation. As Sir Ken says, finding your Element 'offers us our best, and perhaps our only promise for genuine and sustainable success in a very uncertain future'.

The Birth of Qualified Tutor

I found my Element in tutoring in the autumn of 2019. I had just finished my National Professional Qualification for Headship (NPQH), and my wonderful father had recently passed away. I was ready to take on a bigger challenge in my career, but I felt sure that a head teacher role in a large school would crush me. I was never a 'career teacher'. All those maternity leaves meant that I had never become institutionalised; I was perfectly happy to disrupt the status quo in service of finding a better way. This worked well in my small community school, but I knew I would never be able to lead change from inside a larger setting.

During my NPQH, I had noticed that all the coaches and facilitators on the course were former school leaders. I realised that there are ways to contribute to education other than working in a school. And I really wanted to contribute.

I had been working away at this problem for months, trying to find a niche in education where I could bring my whole self. I reflected on my strengths, on what I had achieved so far and on what made me feel excited and inspired to go to work.

As a school leader, I had always focused on developing the adults to improve outcomes for the students. I would do everything I could to advocate for my staff, from ensuring we had a world-class crèche to enabling training routes for non-qualified teachers. I was able to establish a culture of professional development in that school that made lasting change.

At that time, my eldest child, Michael, was in a failing high school and desperately in need of tuition. He wanted to study science at university, but was beginning to worry that he wouldn't get the chance because of the disruptive behaviour in his class. Of course, I needed to help him, so I started the search for a tutor.

I quickly discovered that finding a tutor isn't difficult at all. In fact, it is all too easy. It is possible for anyone to set themselves up as a tutor in minutes. Registering with some online platforms is as easy as ordering takeout. The entry points to tutoring are so poorly guarded that it is hard for a parent to know what to expect.

It occurred to me that the insecurity I had felt as a tutor was matched by the parents' insecurity in choosing a tutor. That is when it landed.

Tutors, as a demographic within the education population, are underdeveloped, underrepresented and underestimated. This makes them insecure and makes parents unsure, all of which undermines the teaching and learning process – and, ultimately, outcomes for students. I would take what I had learned on the NPQH and develop a qualification for tutors.

I began to research social enterprises and community-based businesses. In Qualified Tutor's first manifesto from December 2019, I wrote:

The Qualified Tutor vision is that all students will have regular opportunities to benefit from direct instruction delivered by trained tutors.

- *By making teacher-training accessible for tutors we will enable more, and more able, tutors to enter the market.*
- *By providing a community platform we will invite tutors to see themselves as professionals, as educators, as change-makers.*

I had found my Element in tutoring. I found a niche that lent itself to my passions and talents, and that aligned with what the world needed and what I felt I could bring. The grassroots, community-based approach to professional development is where I thrive. I love to bring people together. I love to raise them up to feel their own worth.

The Qualified Tutor professional development community now provides training and qualifications, community and events, and credentials and certification to the tutoring profession. The workshops you will cover in Part II of this book are based on the Foundations of Effective Tutoring course, which has now been taken by thousands of tutors from all walks of life. We created World Tutors' Day (2 July) and the Love Tutoring Festivals, which are a series of free events designed to inspire and delight the tutoring profession. Our mission is to 'raise standards in tutoring, together' and, in doing so, to bring clarity to a very complex profession, thereby addressing the systemic lack of confidence in tutoring.

What I have learned since then is that the world is full of lost and lonely tutors and would-be tutors, like I was, working in siloes, unconnected and uninspired. Many of them still don't realise that there is a better way. Through Qualified Tutor membership and the Love Tutoring message, I have been able to gather together these tutors and ensure they have the infrastructure they need to do their best work for all our young people. It is emotionally exhausting but incredibly rewarding work. I hope you will consider joining us.

Safe, Skilled and Supported

Let's go back again to me as a young mum tutoring in her kitchen – or maybe to a version of you in a similar moment at your laptop in your loft or garden room – gazing out the window, listless and lonely. What did we need to love tutoring?

For me, I didn't need a boss, but I did need guidance. I needed to know what good looks like in tutoring. I needed a definition of excellence that was expansive, not reductive. I needed to see a progression route to inspire me to stick around, to become an expert and to build a lasting, viable career in tutoring. I needed to know how to be the tutor my student needs.

This is hard for me to say – being equal parts nerd and rebel, I am naturally anti-authoritarian, as many of us are in tutoring – but the openness and flexibility of tutoring is a mixed blessing. On the one hand, the fact that tutors aren't hemmed in by external regulations enables us to be agile and responsive to students' changing needs. We can take them outside or off-topic as we see fit. On the other hand, that same openness means that it is terribly hard to know what good looks like, and that is the root of our problem.

Tutors, individually and as a whole profession, need to opt in to a meaningful quality assurance process to enable tutors and clients to choose each other with confidence. This doesn't need to be a top-down movement. I am proposing a grassroots approach to raising standards in tutoring. If we were heart surgeons, bridge builders or train drivers, quality assurance would be baked into everything we do. Is the profession of tutoring any less high stakes? We heal hearts, build bridges and drive learning daily. We are working with vulnerable students, anxious students and determined students at the most critical moments in their academic careers. They, and the people who care for them, reach out to tutors for help. To be worthy of such a privilege, we must approach tutoring responsibly.

We all need tutoring to be successful and sustainable. Unregulated tutoring isn't right for the tutor or for the student. For tutoring to become a trusted part of the educational landscape, it needs to grow up.

Whilst there are too few accountability measures in place within tutoring, many educational professionals believe that teaching currently has more than enough. I am not suggesting that we accept the accountability agenda that defines the modern education system. No longer willing to defer to the judgement of teachers, schools are riddled with checks and balances to evaluate and standardise teaching. More data drops and assessment points are introduced each year. To know whether you have taught a subject well you need to be a data analyst. Most tutors resented being made to jump through hoops in schools and workplaces. Many of us left the schools or offices where we worked because we were sick of the bureaucracy.

Tutors don't need more red tape. We need professionalism. A peer-reviewed and approved system that assures quality without reducing individuality. I believe that we simply need to establish a flexible and meaningful set of professional standards that will allow us to do our best work and against which we can hold ourselves accountable.

After years of trying to squeeze tutoring to fit in with teaching standards, I eventually came up with a model that felt flexible and inclusive enough to include all types of tutors and simple enough for the families with whom they work to quickly comprehend. I realised that it came down to just three core principles. In order to be the tutor your student needs, you need to be safe, you need to be skilled and you need to be supported.

It is only when these three principles are in place that we are able to ask questions, do our best work, and grow together. Without them, we are too anxious and too insecure to move ahead and make progress. Throughout this book we will explore how being safe, skilled and supported can transform your tutoring.

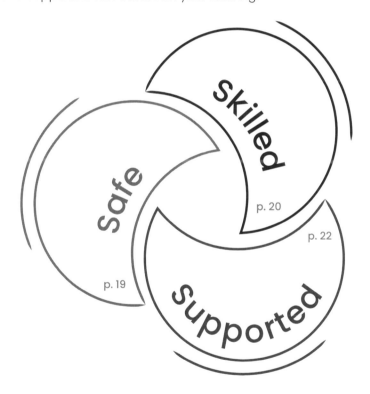

In fact, we all need to feel safe, skilled and supported in every role we take on. If we had felt safe, skilled and supported in the classroom, many of us wouldn't have left mainstream education. But that is another conversation for another day.

In order to
be the tutor
your student
needs, you
need to be
safe, you
need to be
skilled and
you need to
be **supported**.

Safe

Of course, your student needs you to be safe; this is non-negotiable. But most tutors I know have never been asked for evidence, not even when registering with an agency. To move away from the Plan B, ad hoc, side hustle mindset, and give yourself and your clients peace of mind, there are some simple but important actions you need to take, and if you haven't done them already, I am going to ask you to do them right now.

Complete this checklist; if you can't answer 'yes' to every single question, I want you to put down this book and go and sort them out before reading on. Are you ready?

 Do you have up-to-date evidence of a clean police record and that you are permitted to work with children? In the UK, this would be an enhanced Disclosure and Barring Service (DBS) check. If you aren't sure what that would be where you are, use whatever is required in your local area for teachers working alone with children as your guideline.

 Do you have up-to-date training in child protection and safeguarding children and vulnerable adults? We will cover this important information in this book, but to gain a certificate you will need to complete a course. You can access this through Qualified Tutor, the National Society for the Prevention of Cruelty to Children (NSPCC) or many other credible training providers. Be sure that the training covers at least the key points covered by your local schools.

 Do you have an insurance policy that protects you and is accurately based on the way you work – for example, professional indemnity, public liability, business contents, employers' liability?

 Do you have policies and procedures in place that lay out your terms and conditions, safeguarding, safer recruitment, where relevant, and data protection compliance?

Do you have a verified way for your clients to give you feedback? Try Trustpilot, Google Reviews or Facebook Reviews. This is the best way of measuring your impact and gathering testimonials against the day when someone accuses you of being anything less than excellent. An independent tutor's reputation can be destroyed by the smallest hint of an allegation of misconduct. Well aware of this, tutors feel vulnerable, and that feeling can be all it takes to ruin a career in tutoring.

Celebration station

If you are reading on, I will assume that you have successfully completed this five-point checklist. If you really want to make my day, email me at julia@qualifiedtutor.com to let me know you have done so. Don't be shy – I really want to hear from you.

Actually, if you close this book now and never pick it up again, I am satisfied that we have both achieved something important. If every tutor had these five fundamentals in place, and if every parent knew to expect them as a minimum, every student would be safer.

Skilled

Your student also needs you to be skilled. As the world of education shifts towards something we can't predict, staying skilled is an ongoing commitment. Keeping up to date with the skills, knowledge and beliefs in all areas of tutoring – from exam specifications to inclusive practice to filing tax returns – is a huge commitment.

Business practices aside, the pedagogy of tutoring is a new area to educational research. Increasingly, there are academic studies coming out exploring what works well in tutoring. To date, most of these have been in relation to integrating tutoring into schools, but passages such as this one from a large meta-study from 2022 are really helpful:

> Strong instruction is **responsive** to each student's existing skill level and focuses on long-term academic goals. Instruction draws on a student's interests and strengths to pique that student's interest and facilitate collaboration. Quality instruction is informed by the tutor's strong **relationships** with their students through which tutors learn about students and their life contexts, applying this knowledge to lesson planning and instruction. Tutors are **personally invested** in the success of their students and have hope for their student's academic progress.[3]

Whilst experienced tutors intuitively develop these strong instructional skills, it can be helpful to articulate them clearly when training new tutors. That is why I created the three keys of effective tutoring model to explain what excellence in tutoring looks like. These three behaviours will unlock the success of any tutor in any subject with any student. When taken together, they enable ongoing success for both you and your student. The three keys of effective tutoring are *relationship*, *responsiveness* and *reflectiveness*.

3   S. White, L. Groom-Thomas and S. Loeb, *Undertaking Complex But Effective Instructional Supports for Students: A Systematic Review of Research on High-Impact Tutoring Planning and Implementation.* EdWorkingPaper 22-652 (2022), p. 44; my emphasis. Available at: https://files.eric.ed.gov/fulltext/ED625876.pdf.

Every great tutor is accomplished in building relationships with the student and their supporting adults. Every great tutor will respond to a student's changing needs in the moment, adapting to optimise learning. Every great tutor will reflect on what went well and what could have gone better, leaning into the gaps to ensure continual improvement.

Part II of this book will help you to really dig into what relationship, responsiveness and reflectiveness look like for you. We will look into the pedagogy of tutoring and how it compares to teaching. Rather than thinking of this book as the answer, I hope you will use it as a jumping-off point for your own research and doing a deep dive into the topics that seem most relevant to you. Committing to ongoing professional development is the best cure for imposter syndrome. It also helps us to model the love of learning we hope to inspire in our students. Being skilled is a lifelong endeavour.

Supported

This one is less obvious, but it's actually where the magic lies. Your student needs you to be supported. The minute we feel supported, we know that we are part of something greater than ourselves. When we build supportive relationships with like-minded tutors, we develop a context within which we can feel safer and become more skilled. We can ask questions, share wins and encourage others. Feeling supported gives us a sense of collective efficacy as part of the wider tutoring profession. In the Qualified Tutor community, members reflect, share and develop in a safe and supportive environment. They grow in confidence, and in their commitment. They grow to love tutoring. As you'll see throughout this book, it is the power of mutual support that gives the tutoring profession its potential for hope and transformation.

Be Curious, Be Generous and Be Reflective

In order to help you to be the tutor your student needs, this book is structured in three parts. Part I will help you to let go of whatever is holding you back. This is what I call the 'Plan B mindset', and it must be recognised and rejected. Part II, the Foundations of Effective Tutoring, will help you to understand what good looks like in tutoring, and how you can achieve it. Part III shows you how to build a career in tutoring you love. By this point, I hope you will have become inspired to find your own Element in tutoring and to participate in the change that needs to happen in education.

In a sense, the three parts of this book represent the canary, the phoenix and the dove from my Preface. Recognising your own sensitivity, building up your resilience and, finally, inspiring you to become a change-maker is the journey of this book. But change cannot happen passively. For this book to lead to lasting change in your life, you will need to do the work.

To that end, I have included some 'pause points' along the way, where I will pose some open-ended questions based on the material we have covered. There are no right answers; they are simply opportunities for you to make the learning relevant to your unique situation. These questions are based on the Qualified Tutor house rules: 'Be Curious', 'Be Generous' and 'Be Reflective'. These three behaviours sum up the culture that underpins everything else.

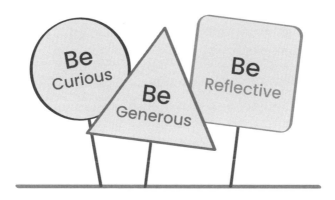

- **Be Curious.** Open your mind to new opportunities and possibilities. This is an invitation for everyone. For experienced tutors, it is a chance to set down what you already know, so your mind is free to explore afresh. For new tutors, it is permission to explore new ideas without judgement or pressure. I have delivered training for tutors far more experienced than myself. Whilst this always feels terrifying at first, I have found that the best of them show up with openness and curiosity, allowing fresh insights to arise. I ask you to do the same.

- **Be Generous.** This means generosity of spirit, to others and to yourself. This is what we are known for at Qualified Tutor, where sharing what we know and giving the benefit of the doubt are the norm. Engage with an abundance mindset; there is more of everything than you need.

- **Be Reflective.** This means being able to examine your motives and how these influence your behaviour. This is where you get to step back and think about how the ideas in this book relate to the way you tutor. Being reflective is the secret sauce in professional development, because unless you let the learning inform your practice, it isn't really development, is it?

I have also included some 'celebration stations' throughout the book. These are places where I ask you to email me to let me know about the progress you are making. As I have said, my Element is helping you to thrive, so please do let me know how you are getting on.

I have seen the lives of tutors transformed by the ideas in this book, and I want the same for you. If you are willing to participate with curiosity, with generosity and with reflectiveness, you will learn to be the tutor your student needs.

Pause Point

Are you willing to engage with the ideas in this book with curiosity, generosity and reflectiveness?

. . . .

. . . .

What are you hoping to gain from the ideas in this book?

. . . .

. . . .

Who will benefit if this book delivers on its promise?

. . . .

. . . .

What would it feel like to really love tutoring?

. . . .

. . . .

Love Tutoring Role Models: Kayleigh Rapson

When I first met Kayleigh at a Love Tutoring Festival in 2020, she was a qualified teacher and special educational needs coordinator (SENDCO). She had just finished her master's degree and was running an early years provision. Although clearly an immensely capable person, she was feeling lost and unsure of herself, which, as you will see, is a theme with Kayleigh.

I knew I wanted to teach, but I didn't think I was capable. I went to university a bit later than everyone else, at about 22. I did my teaching degree and had such a good time because university makes you think that anything is possible. Then I went into school and all that magic was lost. It wasn't a nice environment.

I had major anxiety all the way through that first year because I was constantly being assessed, constantly being told I wasn't good enough. Even when I'd had an outstanding observation, I came out of the meeting crying. I was really ill during that year, so I decided, 'Actually, I'm not going back to the classroom. I'm going to give in my notice. That's enough primary school for me.'

Kayleigh went back to her roots, working in an early years setting and working her way up to becoming a SENDCO and manager:

I worked with families who were very early on in their diagnosis and treatments. Often, I was the one having those difficult conversations with parents as well as putting in interventions. I also managed a lot of staff. The nursery that I went to was run by teachers who had come out of the system. We called it a 'teacher haven' because we took on broken teachers, and we all thrived.

When COVID-19 struck in 2020, and Kayleigh was furloughed, she volunteered as a tutor:

The only thing that didn't sit right with me in tutoring was that I come from quite a poor background. We could never afford tutors when I was younger. I was working with some quite well-off families and the children weren't in difficulty. They didn't actually need me. It was just to get ahead of the game. It was the families that had the children with special needs that I needed to be with. I realised that's where my heart was – with kids who needed a bit of extra support, extra guidance, extra love.

When Kayleigh popped into our online Love Tutoring Festival, she didn't know what to expect:

Everything you were saying was exactly how I felt about education. I was feeling lost. I didn't know what I wanted to do. As much as I would have loved to stay in early years, there's no future: you get to management and then that's it. I'm someone who likes to progress, to get better and do more.

Love Tutoring showed me this completely new way of working and this whole almost hidden realm of adjacent teaching that you don't really see unless you're in it. It made me realise what I wanted from life, and that was to create opportunities for children. I went away and did some more homework, stayed with Qualified Tutor and sought other ways to broaden my clientele. I realised that alternative provision would probably be for me.

Kayleigh had finally found her Element. She launched Bright Sparks Education and put a bid in for alternative provision work with West Sussex County Council. However, things didn't go to plan: 'Just as we were getting the okay from the local authority, I got pregnant. We hadn't thought that we would get pregnant because we were having difficulties. We thought, "We'll shelve that – let's concentrate on the business." And then, obviously, that's when it happens!'

True to form, Kayleigh did as much planning for her maternity leave as she possibly could, but her business didn't thrive whilst she was away:

In my haste, I asked the wrong people to step in. It was a really scary time because I thought, 'Everything I've built, I'm going to lose,' because I want to be at home with my baby, but I also have my heart in this business. Then my sister-in-law stepped in. She just was perfect for the role. We changed the company and put loads of work in to our senior leadership team.

Having saved her business, Kayleigh was then able to realise an even bigger dream. She found her first premises:

One of my dreams was to have a space because all our children were very isolated in their homes. I felt that, even if they weren't working with other children, if they came into a centre, that would help them to expand their world a little bit.

We used a very 'early years' approach in that hub. We introduced a sensory room. We introduced role play. We introduced messy play. We now have another space, which is right next door to the hub, where we have three classrooms, a science lab and a cooking space.

We also have our own drivers to escort the children in and out of the community. Basically, we have our own mini school going on, and it's absolutely wonderful. We're planning to start up a summer club so that we can continue to support and to serve the community.

We don't offer more than fifteen hours of education per week. We can offer up to eighteen hours without being inspected by Ofsted. We don't want to be inspected because we feel that it would restrict what we can offer the children.

Four years on, Kayleigh owns two alternative provision centres serving thirty-five students with special educational needs. She employs five staff members as well as deploying thirty self-employed tutors. She has more than exceeded her salary as an early years manager and is serving a real need in her community on the south coast of England.

My aim has always been to make our community a better place for neurodivergent children. We all know that the world is not set up for neurodiverse children or neurodiverse people. We want to make it that little bit easier to access, so we need the staff in place to support those interactions and to take them out. We don't hide the children away; they are often out and about, and use the centre as a base.

Kayleigh is a natural leader of people, and watching her grow in confidence has been incredibly rewarding. She told me:

You have to make sure that the people you're employing are, as you say, safe, skilled and supported. You have to make sure you're on top of the training. You have to put in the commitment and the time. It won't be lucrative at the beginning, but as you make yourself and what you can offer to the community known, then the rest of it comes. It's a big learning curve. We're learning all the time. I couldn't ask for anything more.

I asked Kayleigh what she knows now that she didn't know when she started out:

When you take that leap and you believe in yourself, when you believe in what you're selling and your ethos as a company, when you go in with your why and you keep that to heart, then you can make really wonderful things happen. I wish I had known at the beginning not to be so worried and not to be so scared. I still have days when I think, 'I'm not cut out to do this. I don't know what I'm doing.' But, actually, I do know what I'm doing, so I make a point of saying, 'No, I am good at my job. I do know what I am doing. I can do this.'

As a Love Tutoring role model, and someone who truly did find her Element and fly as a tutor, Kayleigh's final message is simply:

Go for it. Find your people. Find your community. Surround yourself with people who believe in you. Surround yourself with people who can offer their emotional support too. It doesn't have to be someone who knows about teaching. You need to find somebody who will champion you. For me, that was my husband. He really supported me. Then I managed to find Qualified Tutor as a community, and that was it. I didn't look back. It just felt right. If it feels right, and if you have your community around you, go for it. That's what I would say.

Chapter 2

EXPLORING (AND EXPLODING) THE MYTHS AND MISCONCEPTIONS OF TUTORING

We live in interesting times for tutors worldwide. In some countries, tutoring has become a panacea for educational disruption, displacement and disadvantage. In others, we have become the pariahs of the education sector, banned and forced underground.

In the UK, tutors are filling staffing gaps and supporting war refugees. Around £4.9 billion has been allocated from government funding to provide COVID-19 'catch-up' support directly to schools in England, including through tutoring.[1] This collision of the public and private sectors is disrupting the status quo of tutoring and forcing the profession to prepare for regulation, quality assurance and accountability. Improved safeguards such as criminal record checks are fast becoming an expectation, thankfully.

The modalities of tutoring have changed beyond recognition. Online marketplaces are now the most common way for students to find

1   House of Commons Committee of Public Accounts, *Education Recovery in Schools in England. Fifty-Fifth Report of Session 2022–23*. HC 998 (22 May 2023), p. 4. Available at: https://publications.parliament.uk/pa/cm5803/cmselect/cmpubacc/998/report.html.

tutors. Improved internet access, video conferencing platforms and social media are making tutors more accessible and affordable for every student. Whilst ten years ago tutoring looked like two people sitting together with a book between them, today it is very often a group of mixed-age, mixed-nationality students gathered in an online room with a tutor they will never meet in person. How exciting is that?

However, even now, there are ideas that persist about tutoring which are holding us back. Some of these ideas will be old news, speaking to the way things used to be. Others will be fake news, speaking to a fear of the unknown. For many reasons, which we will look at together, the optics of tutoring are still not great. To improve this, and embrace our profession, we need to explore and, yes, to explode some pernicious and pervasive myths about tutoring.

Misconception 1: I Know What a Tutor Looks Like

Twenty years ago, tutoring was a specialised local marketplace regulated by a small and powerful client base. It was a safety net, a failsafe for the children of the wealthy. Tutors relied on word-of-mouth referrals. The names of the best in the business were guarded jealously or whispered by parents like a secret password – or, perhaps, a secret weapon.

In those days, there were four main tutor archetypes: the governess, the teacher/tutor, the boy-next-door and the gatekeeper. Each one had a specific role and a clearly delineated relationship with students and parents based on perceived authority and power. If you wanted to be a tutor, you had to fall into one of these categories, you had to work with families who could afford you, you had to know your place and you had to get results.

The *governess* was a uniquely positioned member of staff in a high-net-worth family. This individual would leverage a good degree at a famous university for a well-paid situation as a live-in tutor, often enjoying the opportunity to travel the world in style. Excellent interpersonal skills were a must.

Melissa Harvey started out as the governess archetype, travelling the world and becoming a highly valued and trusted member of the family. Melissa built long-lasting relationships, and has stayed in touch with her students for decades, becoming a mentor for life.

The *teacher/tutor* had an air of experience and authority. This type of tutor was reassuring, and sometimes reassuringly scary, to the parents as well as the children. Formal and proper, they used old-school teaching approaches to mimic the school experience in comfortable kitchens and studies. Depending on whether the student needed a totally different approach or simply more of the same, this type of tutoring either really helped the child or really didn't.

I fell into this category of tutor (except the scary bit). Parents trusted me because I was in tune with what was happening and expected in schools. I used familiar jargon, resources and approaches, adjusting them in the moment to the needs of the student.

The *boy-next-door* was at the opposite end of the career path. He was an unpretentious high-schooler who did well in his exams. He was relatable, passionate about his subject and excited to make a difference in the world. He started out helping family friends and quickly worked out that tutoring was more comfortable than a newspaper round.

Johnny Manning, founder of Manning's Tutors, is a long-haired, left-wing entrepreneur who started out as the boy-next-door maths tutor in his village. Local parents took good care of him, with each student's family driving him from their house to the next one, with the final family of the evening giving him dinner before dropping him back home.

The last of the traditional tutor archetypes is the *gatekeeper*. Whether it is private school entrance exams, Law School Admission Tests or Oxbridge interview preparation, these tutors have the techniques, knowledge and connections to give students their best shot at crossing a threshold. Traditionally, gatekeepers with the best track records were treated with awe. They were the maestros and divas of the tutoring world, commanding high rates and fierce loyalty.

Anita Oberoi is an 11+ entrance exam tutor. Her students are under a great deal of pressure to succeed, and so is Anita. But she does things differently. Remembering the pressure she felt as a student taking the 11+ years ago, she is determined to create a different experience for her students. It is a high-stakes niche, but Anita is determined to support children's mental health and well-being as well as their academic outcomes.

Today, the tutoring sector looks very different to how it did when you and I grew up. The lines have blurred between the four archetypes and many more have sprung up in-between. Whilst there is still plenty of in-person, one-to-one tutoring happening, a wide variety of other delivery models now exist.

Parents and students rely on tutors for all sorts of support they can't get, or can't get enough of, in the classroom. Some tutors have a wealth of professional experience to draw on, and others are only one or two years ahead of the students. Some tutor online, following time zones to be able to teach throughout the day. Some support home-schoolers or follow world-schoolers on their travels, either physically or online. Tutors can now be found in every strand of the education landscape. We each have our specialism, and we are each as unique as the students we support.

Misconception 2: Tutoring is Only for the Most Privileged

The press loves to get its teeth into tutoring. Divisive headlines and articles about tutoring featuring phrases like 'parental hothousing', 'the wild west of the education landscape' or 'fuelling the educational arms race' are reductive and dismissive of all the hard-working, caring people in our space. Society may fear a decentralised education model, but this might be precisely why tutoring can be so effective.

Maybe it is the nebulous nature of the profession that leaves tutors open to such stigma, or perhaps it is the implication of elitism. Whatever the reason, the press, on the left and the right, keep the tutor on the outside. Rather than fearing an educational arms race, why don't we celebrate the support on offer and boost subsidies for the least advantaged students to access the same support as their peers? Surely, our social responsibility is to close gaps by raising up the less advantaged rather than disabling the rest?

Over the past three decades, a succession of researchers, school leaders and change-makers working separately and, increasingly, together have pushed for change in education. Developments in neuroscience have accentuated two interconnected themes: inclusion and research-informed practice. As a result, we are now using a data-led approach to what works best in teaching to ensure that we provide a more effective educational experience to more of our young people.

Whilst there have been the inevitable fads and flip-flops along the way, the consistent drive towards inclusive, evidence-driven practice means there is now a vast body of work informing policymakers. One of the most comprehensive and accessible resources is the Education Endowment Foundation's Teaching and Learning Toolkit.[2] The toolkit evaluates a wide range of interventions that schools can deploy to support disadvantaged learners. It measures impact in months of progress against cost and strength of evidence. The data point to what educationalists call 'best bets' in what will work for students; there are no guarantees because the variables are so complex. Although the toolkit isn't perfect, it has been a game-changer for policymakers and school leaders looking to make evidence-based budget decisions since 2011.

According to the Education Endowment Foundation, the headline news is that well-delivered one-to-one tuition can improve student outcomes by five months. In addition, many of the other

2   See https://educationendowmentfoundation.org.uk/education-evidence/ teaching-learning-toolkit/one-to-one-tuition.

high-ranking interventions – such as feedback, self-regulation, metacognition and mastery learning – are all features of effective tutoring. Furthermore, small group tuition (which the toolkit cites as potentially more useful since it provides four months' progress for significantly less cost than one-to-one tuition) can also incorporate peer tutoring, collaborative learning, individualised interventions, and social and emotional learning. The fact is that tutoring is an opportunity that should be made available to every student.

Lee Elliot Major, one of the creators of the toolkit and the first professor of social mobility at the University of Exeter, collaborated on a paper in 2020 calling for a 'National Tutoring Service' to level the playing field and enable less-privileged students' access to free tutoring.[3] This gave rise to a National Tutoring Programme (NTP) in England and a £1 billion COVID-19 catch-up initiative; in the following years, countries across the world, including the United States and the Netherlands, have followed suit.

Since the beginning of the NTP in November 2020, almost five million courses of tuition have been delivered in 36% of state schools in England. Despite these impressive numbers, and the willingness of the tutoring sector to adapt swiftly to fulfil demand, it is significant that more than half of schools chose not to use the funding at all.[4] Teachers feared whether the tutoring would be of sufficient quality to justify the cost of administering the programme. There were concerns around how much would be subsidised and how much the school would still need to pay. There were also criticisms of how top-down the approach was initially, leading to an adjustment to give school leaders more power to choose the tutoring provision. In short, it was a complex beast of an initiative.

The NTP received a great deal of criticism. The education sector is typically suspicious of new ideas, especially when those ideas rely on an efficient interface between the public and private sectors.

3   L. E. Major, E. Tyers and R. Chu, The National Tutoring Service: Levelling-Up Education's Playing Field (2020). Available at: https://www.exeter.ac.uk/media/universityofexeter/collegeofsocialsciencesandinternationalstudies/education/documentsfordownload/National_Tutoring_Service_April_2020.pdf.
4   See National Tutoring Programme (Academic Year 2023/24). Available at: https://explore-education-statistics.service.gov.uk/find-statistics/national-tutoring-programme.

Learning to deploy tutors placed an extra administrative burden on school management at a time when they were overwhelmed, facing the first COVID-19 variants and learning to teach online. Everything felt surreal.

Whilst it wasn't an ideal time to launch a new tutoring scheme, there were bright spots which suggest that the legacy of the NTP in schools could be long-lasting and helpful. Stephen Fraser, who was deputy chief executive of the Education Endowment Foundation when it launched the programme, told me that, ideally, 'tutoring will become another instrument in the orchestra of school'. Whilst historically tutoring has been accessible only to the most privileged, as we broaden the definition of tutoring to include small group, online and in-school interventions, alternative provision, education other than at school, academic coaching and all manner of extracurricular instruction for both adults and children, the community of tutors is becoming broader, richer and far more inclusive.

Online schools are a perfect example of this, where a broad education is made accessible to young people who are unable to attend school. Kirstin Coughtrie, founder of Gaia Learning, an online school for neurodiverse learners, offers a guided provision tailored to the unique needs of each learner. As a neurodiverse person herself, Kirstin knows that it is imperative that we inspire these learners with strategies and opportunities to thrive on their own terms.

So, is tutoring only for the most privileged? Not any more. Inclusivity must be woven into the fabric of the tutoring profession. We must include the students who aren't managing in the mainstream. The stack 'em high model might be suitable for commodities like tea and coffee, but it isn't acceptable for people. Nor is it effective. It is no longer sufficient to say that we can't afford to give students more personalised input. It is now time to assert that we can't afford not to; the collateral damage to our young people is too great. The times they are a-changin'. Wherever there is a student who isn't getting what they need at school, there is a tutor, somewhere in the world, who is willing to help. Going forward, tutoring is for everyone.

Inclusivity **must be woven into the fabric** of the tutoring profession.

Misconception 3: Tutors Must Be Qualified Teachers

Not all teachers make great tutors, and not all great tutors are qualified teachers. In fact, two of my favourite tutors, both of whom have supported my own children, don't have teaching qualifications.

Georgina Green is a scientist who worked for GlaxoSmithKline. She escaped the bureaucracy of the pharmaceutical industry to set up a science, technology, engineering and mathematics (STEM) tuition agency. Green Tutors now has a decade of expertise in providing excellent science tuition and study skills at GCSE and A level. Georgina told me that her hope is for 'every child to grow in confidence and passion, to learn without barriers, without anxiety and without exams ruining the whole process'.

Helen Osmond is a maths tutor who had to put her teaching degree on hold for personal reasons ten years ago. As a young mum, she started tutoring to keep her hand in until she could finish her studies and become a 'proper teacher'. Years on, she says that the thought of going back to the classroom instead of maintaining Osmond Education, her thriving tutoring business, seems truly ridiculous. Helen says: 'I'm a confidence builder with my students. They come to me anxious and lacking in confidence in maths, and I work with them so they approach the maths without the panic they started with. It is the "I get it!" and "It's not so bad!" moments that make it so rewarding.'

Helen and Georgina are two of the most capable tutors I know. They are organised and focused experts in their subjects, and they have each been tutoring for years. They know their niche, they connect generously with other tutors and they are always looking for ways to build their skills and knowledge.

It isn't always easy, of course. Not having a teaching qualification has left them each feeling somehow 'less than' in the past. Most newly qualified teachers who tutor for an hour or two at the weekend will have far less expertise than either Helen or Georgina, but they have the teaching qualification and that somehow counts for more.

Together, in this book, we will find out how Georgina and Helen have embraced a love of tutoring by ensuring that they are safe, skilled and supported, and how you can do the same.

Misconception 4: Tutoring Means the Teacher Has Failed

Tutoring isn't a sign of a teacher's failure. On the contrary, it can be a sign of their great success.

One of my children, Daniel, had such a hard time in his first primary school that surviving each day was an achievement. His class was too large and incredibly disruptive. His teachers were inexperienced and the school leadership was insufficient. He hadn't made progress in the classroom because he hadn't felt safe. He wasn't supported and directed by able professionals. Daniel was failing to thrive. I knew I needed to move him, but there were no places available in any of the local schools.

Bolstering Daniel's sense of self was the priority. Learning was a million miles away at that time. Although he was working more than two years below expectations for his age, there was no point in bringing in a tutor because Daniel just wasn't ready to learn.

The week Daniel was accepted into his new school was the same week the first COVID-19 lockdown began. Surprisingly, it was the best thing that could have happened for him. He was able to rest at home, detoxing from a dysfunctional school environment and slowly getting used to his new classmates via remote learning. He rode his bike, played in the paddling pool and completed less than 50% of what the new school asked of him. In my mind it was a huge success.

Once the restrictions eased and he was back in the classroom, Daniel was able to adjust to his new surroundings. He began to accept that people cared about him. The staff were genuinely ambitious for his progress. In fact, they were relentlessly rigorous and pushy. I was so grateful that, finally, someone was telling Daniel that he was capable of more and better. His new teachers never once let him off the hook. They showed him that they expected him to succeed, and they were consistent in their approach. If he didn't bring in his homework, he did it in school. If he couldn't access the work, someone sat down and helped him.

Daniel's determined teachers raised his expectations of himself. They introduced a value for hard work and its associated effort. The noise in his head calmed down and he felt safe enough to learn.

Once he had completed a full year at his new school, Daniel was ready for intervention. I called Alyson Burns, an ex-head teacher who had left her school to become a full-time dyslexia specialist teacher and assessor. She is very firm but very warm. Daniel and Alyson play all sorts of literacy games together, and he is finally making progress, and enjoying the journey.

Misconception 5: Tutoring Means the Parents Have Failed

Attitudes towards tutoring vary greatly in different cultures across the UK and the globe.[5] In some families parents employ tutors as a badge of honour, in some it is a glass floor ensuring that students can't fall too far, and in others tutoring is simply a necessary expense. What we do know is that most parents would pay for tutoring if they could afford it.[6]

---

5   The Sutton Trust found that 'Black and Asian pupils were more than twice as likely to have ever received private tutoring (50% and 55%), compared to White pupils (24%). 46% of pupils in London had received private tutoring, compared to 30% for England as a whole': C. Cullinane and R. Montacute, *Tutoring – The New Landscape: Recent Trends in Private and School-Based Tutoring* (London: Sutton Trust, 2023), p. 3. Available at: https://www.suttontrust.com/our-research/tutoring-2023-the-new-landscape.

6   Most parents '(64%) cited cost as a barrier for accessing more tutoring for their child': S. Burtonshaw and J. Simons, *The Future of Tutoring* (London: Public First, 2023), p. 23. Available at: https://www.impetus.org.uk/assets/publications/The-Future-of-Tutoring.pdf.

My wonderful business partner, Odette Wohlman, reflects on a time when she was spending more than a thousand pounds a month on tutors for her four children. They were struggling to keep up in school, which was affecting their self-esteem and therefore their behaviour. This negative cycle made the whole family feel trapped. 'I was so desperate to get it right,' she says. Feeling vulnerable and overwhelmed, she did what she could to help her children.

It can be difficult for parents to understand the school system – to interpret school reports and teacher talk – but most know their children and are determined to do the right thing for them. Employing a tutor might be one of the best things a parent can do for their child. But finding the right tutor isn't simple, and the really tricky part is that there is usually only one chance to get it right.

If I engage the wrong tutor for my child, it could adversely affect both their results and their confidence. Just as a great tutor is inspiring and enabling, a less-than-great tutor can be disappointing and disheartening. Even as an experienced teacher and tutor myself, I still find selecting a tutor stressful.[7]

I like to compare choosing a tutor to shoe shopping. Most parents I know will spend more on a well-fitting pair of shoes than on any other item of clothing. When my kids were little, everything they wore was hand-me-downs – except their shoes, which were sensible, hard-wearing and expertly fitted. No unsupportive ballet pumps or glittery flip-flops for my kids' growing feet. Boring, I know, but responsible too.

Just as picking shoes for your child requires a nuanced understanding of the needs of those young feet at their age, stage and season, so choosing a tutor requires a good knowledge of the child and their unique profile as a learner.

Whenever I contact a new tutor for one of my children, I usually give them way too much information. But I feel that it is important to be as honest and open as possible, and I learn a great deal from how

7   This is why I have created digital credentials for members of Qualified Tutor – to make it easier for parents to choose with confidence.

the tutor responds. They don't need to have all the answers, but they do need to care enough to listen.

One of my boys, Michael, was facing GCSEs in a failing school when COVID-19 struck and the UK went into lockdown. Michael has a natural aptitude for science and felt disappointed and disenchanted with what was on offer from his teachers. Chris Wright, a 63-year-old ex-army-colonel-turned-tech-entrepreneur-turned-science-teacher, worked online with Michael for four hours per week on maths, biology, chemistry and physics.

Initially, this felt like an extravagance, but during lockdown those daily sessions with Chris became the touchstone in Michael's schedule. As a mother, I was reassured that for at least one hour a day, Michael was having a sensible conversation with an encouraging adult. Home life during those months was stressful for everyone, and I was grateful to know that Chris was able to keep an eye on Michael.

Far from a sign of failure, finding the right tutor (not to mention getting the child to show up to each session) is a huge achievement. It feels like a bond between parent and child – a way to reassure, rebuild trust and provide support. It can leave you feeling like a minor superhero, with 'I Helped My Child' emblazoned across your hooded sweatshirt!

Misconception 6: Needing a Tutor Means the Student Has Failed

To explain this most hurtful misconception, I like to use the analogy of personal fitness. I'm not great at working out. Put me in a gym and I tremble. I stand at the entrance, feeling intimidated and helpless, in exercise clothes that are really pyjamas and without a clue about how to proceed. The machines are scary, the smell is foreign and everyone else seems so confident.

Me standing panicked at the threshold of a gym is like many anxious children in the classroom. Lurking on the periphery or, worse, hiding in plain sight. Petrified that the next question is coming their way. Tensed up in anticipation of someone bumping their arm, knocking their chair or raising their voice. Horrified that the child next to them can see their empty page, their poor handwriting or spelling errors.

The classroom fits so few children. For some the work is too hard and for others too easy. The teacher goes too quickly or too slowly. The other students are distracting – too much fun or too scary. Sometimes it is all of the above in a single lesson.

Is a student a failure if they can't follow the learning in the classroom? If they don't understand? If they are too distracted? Am I failing if I can't cope in the gym? Not necessarily. It all depends on what I do next.

In May 2019, I discovered that with a personal trainer I can work out. When I have someone to guide me, to plan around my needs and hold me accountable, I can get fit.

I went to Libby's studio at the back of her garden twice a week. She worked with me and helped me to build strength and confidence. The time and space with Libby was about much more than physical training; it was also self-care. It was a tough time in my life, during the period when my father passed away. He was ill with cancer and left us at the end of that summer. I took a month off, but it made more sense to let Libby support me than to walk away. It was a calm and safe space. And, yes, I did punch out a lot of pain in her boxing gloves. Libby let me choose the music. She knew exactly how to adjust the pace when she could see that I was low or angry or hyper. She didn't let me push my body too hard, nor did she let me coast. Libby was my 'person' at that time of need. She showed up for me and kept me breathing when I felt I had lost my anchor. So many tutors do this every day for their students, in both the most extreme scenarios and the most mundane.

Our students come to believe that they should be able to cope in the classroom 'like everyone else'. But even for those children who are coping and making progress, mainstream education can feel still like running on sand. It is exhausting and heavy going.

The classroom is such a complex learning environment, it is no wonder that some students can't flourish. In fact, it is a wonder that any of them can.

Imagine a group of thirty people at the gym, let's say it is a spinning class, and one trainer trying to cover the room. Each participant in the group has a different set of needs. One person has a weak knee and another has a weak heart. One has incredible speed but not much stamina. Another has all the stamina but forgot her trainers.

In an adult context, we rely on the participants to take care of their own needs, to stop if it gets too much or to remember to wear their knee brace. But often children don't know how to ask for help, and we don't teach them to listen to their inner voice. Instead, we communicate that they should be able to do this. No matter what the starting point. No matter whether they remembered their trainers.

Returning to our fitness metaphor, the spinners who get injured or left behind quite quickly stop coming to class. They might not be honest about it; they may find that they aren't feeling well next Tuesday or have an important work assignment. If they are really resilient, they will find a class that suits them better, but they will definitely find a way to avoid being in the same situation again.

Children in the classroom learn to avoid uncomfortable situations, too, but they don't have such an easy escape route. One of my children used to find a reason to visit the school secretary every day. He would complain that his head hurt, or he needed to call home because he had forgotten his lunch, or he had torn his trousers. Anything for a chance to stretch his legs and get some fresh air. He still struggles to attend school full time nearly a decade later.

Our students aren't failing; the system is failing them. Seeking support is an effective strategy, a sign of resilience and a signal of hope.

Misconception 7: Tutors Are Failed Teachers

Schools are an exciting but sometimes overwhelming work environment. The number of individual interactions a teacher has in school on any given day can be in the thousands.[8] When you amplify that by the number of group interactions – that is, interactions within a class or classes and with students from other classes – it could be tens of thousands. Add to this interactions with colleagues, parents and support staff, and it is incredibly stimulating and intensely exhausting.

All of this is fine if you are in excellent health, pumped with marathon-level energy and in a school brimming with mutual respect and collaboration. The problem is that maintaining a healthy culture in the face of all the daily pressures is just too difficult for many school leaders. The result is that school environments can become toxic very quickly, sometimes with tragic results.

In 2023, head teacher Ruth Perry took her own life after a particularly nasty Ofsted inspection. Unfortunately, there are several known cases where staff have died by suicide due to stress at school.[9] It is no one person's fault in particular, but it is everyone's fault for allowing such a situation to persist.

Many of us cannot and will not work in an endlessly high-pressure school environment. For us, tutoring is a better, healthier and more sustainable way to teach. Most of the tutors I have interviewed tell the same story: they didn't feel sufficiently supported, they didn't feel valued and they didn't feel respected.

---

8   Philip Jackson wrote in his 1990 book *Life in Classrooms* that elementary teachers have 200 to 300 of these determination generating exchanges with students every hour (between 1,200–1,800 a day).

9   A. Fazackerley, Revealed: Stress of Ofsted Inspections Cited as Factor in Deaths of 10 Teachers, *The Observer* (25 March 2023). Available at: https://www.theguardian.com/education/2023/mar/25/revealed-stress-of-ofsted-inspections-cited-as-factor-in-deaths-of-10-teachers.

Misconception 8: Tutors Don't Make Enough Money

Rysia Connolly, science tutor and creator of The Tutor Toolkit, runs online science groups for seven and a half hours per week – and she makes more money than she ever did as a full-time teacher. With up to ten students in a group and two sessions every evening, Monday to Wednesday, Rysia brings in at least £2,000 per week before tax. Rysia doesn't work during school holidays or weekends and she doesn't do one-to-one tutoring (except on an ad hoc basis for those already in one of her groups). As Rysia says, it is 'my business and my rules'.

Rysia is a smart cookie. She spends her days working *on* her business and her evenings working *in* her business. Naturally entrepreneurial, she had already started marketing her group tuition model within months of leaving the classroom. She presents herself flawlessly and makes it look easy. To give you a sense of what that means: her marketing message is so good and her social media presence so coherent that parents will book their children in for group tuition without even communicating directly with her. No interview, no email communication, just a sign-up form. Parents feel that they know what she is about and how she will help their child just by reading her website or following her social media posts. It has taken Rysia years of work to refine her model and learn how to communicate it to her ideal customer.

Rysia now teaches other tutors to do what she does. Once she had maxed out her available tutoring hours, found an hourly rate she was happy with and accommodated as many groups as she could, the next route to giving herself a raise was developing a passive income. It is a misnomer, of course; there is nothing passive about a passive income. Rysia's coaching programme includes an online course, live workshops, a facilitated Facebook group and open access to her via WhatsApp.

She told me that people were reaching out to her online and asking her to teach them how she had done it, so she built The Tutor

Toolkit Academy where she teaches tutors how to develop viable businesses. Her next step will be to train as a coach so she can continue to support the next generation of tutors coming through. By offering to be the 'coach in your pocket', Rysia is building herself up as she builds up the people around her. It is a testament to her own professional journey from the classroom to a successful business owner.

You will encounter many stories like Rysia's throughout this book – examples of tutors who have found new ways of making money that suit their needs and align with their values. Having said all this, tutors tend to be people who are out-of-the-box and a little bit rebellious. We tend to be willing to embrace a life of service and meaning. Money is just a by-product of a good job well done.

· ·

This chapter has been like pulling off a plaster. Bringing some of the stigma out into the light is both painful and intensely satisfying. Now that we have removed it, we can roll up our sleeves and get to grips with becoming the tutor our students need.

 Pause Point

Which of these myths and misconceptions have been holding you back? Are there others, not listed here, that play on your mind?

· ·

· ·

How have the myths and misconceptions of tutoring affected you personally?

....

....

What can you do to release yourself from the myths and misconceptions that are holding you back?

....

....

We would **never** **tolerate** such self-doubt in our students, so **why** do we allow it in ourselves?

Chapter 3

WHAT MIGHT BE HOLDING YOU BACK FROM CREATING A FUTURE IN TUTORING YOU LOVE?

'I don't know what I'm doing.'

'They're going to realise I'm a fraud any minute now.'

'Tutoring isn't a real job.'

We would never tolerate such self-doubt in our students, so why do we allow it in ourselves?

If a student came to me and said, 'I'm rubbish at maths. I'm the worst in the class and my parents think I'm a failure,' I would make it my mission to help them to believe in themselves. This is how I feel towards you.

We cause so much of our own pain. Our limiting beliefs become self-fulfilling, and we remain trapped in the reality we believe we see. We feel weak, so people think we are weak. We feel ashamed, so we shrink back. We feel so isolated that we forget how to reach out to others.

I would like your permission to point out some things you may be doing that are reinforcing your discomfort as a tutor. I would like to show you what might be happening that entrenches you in your negative feelings towards tutoring. And I would like to help you to just stop.

I once heard psychologist Dicken Bettinger illustrate self-defeating behaviour with this story. It starts like a joke, but it isn't funny at all. A man walked into a doctor's office and said, 'My head hurts.' The doctor looked up from the man's files and was amazed to see that he had a hammer in his hand and was hitting himself on the side of the head. No wonder his head hurt! The doctor gently lifted the hammer out of his hand, and the man went away feeling much better.[1]

It isn't that the doctor was an incredible physician; it is just that he was able to see the hammer. The moment we see our insecurities clearly, we are more able to free ourselves of them. This isn't to say that we won't slip back into old habits, but at least we can become more aware of our triggers. There is the possibility of putting down the hammer.

If you have read this far, then perhaps some of the feelings I have described have resonated with you. It is helpful to take responsibility for the part we play in allowing tutoring to feel like a Plan B option. But it is also important to know that our personal experience of tutoring is caused largely by what is happening out there. We have seen that the development of tutoring has been stymied and stunted by the private sector, which is happy to keep tutors siloed and tutoring unregulated. We have taken a good look at the stigma we face as a profession, and we are no longer happy to live in the shadows.

Now that tutoring has been claimed by the mainstream education sector on a macro level, through initiatives such as the NTP, it is time for us to reclaim tutoring at the micro level. But we need to do the work if we are going to love tutoring. It is time to start plotting a course towards a new way of tutoring. Tutoring that you can be proud of and in which you feel you are progressing. Tutoring that pays the bills and gives you the professional satisfaction you

1   Dicken Bettinger, Life 2.0 Innate Health Conference, London, 13–15 May 2018.

crave. Tutoring that really makes a difference for both you and your students.

Stop Doubting Your Expertise

Self-doubt can be crippling, but it can also be galvanising. The best solution to imposter syndrome is to skill up. Learn your craft. Engage in continuous professional development. Reflect on what went well and what could go better. Work with a mentor to analyse your practice objectively. Steven Bartlett, in his book *The Diary of a CEO*, says: 'Those who hoard gold have riches for a moment. Those who hoard knowledge and skills have riches for a lifetime. True prosperity is what you know and can do.'[2]

You don't need a PhD in maths to tutor high school maths, and nor do you need a degree from a famous university. In fact, a PhD might be the last thing your student needs you to have. The 'curse of the expert' points to the idea that it is hard for an expert to remember what it felt like to be a novice. For example, most of us have trouble recalling what it felt like to learn to read. Mastery can make us insensitive to our students' difficulties. We can struggle to empathise as they grapple with a task that looks easy to us.

There is a view that you don't have to be an expert to teach; you only need to be one step ahead. This simply isn't true. If you are only one lesson ahead of your students, you aren't really leading their learning because you don't know where it is going next. Also, you can't know your topic well enough to expand on it, deepen the thinking and go off-curriculum, which most students relish.

What we really need is pedagogical content knowledge. We need to become an expert in the teaching of our subject, or at least to make a start. We need to know the common misconceptions that many students will have with a particular topic and the foundational prerequisites they will need to be able to go forward. Knowing how

. . . .

2   S. Bartlett, *The Diary of a CEO: The 33 Laws of Business and Life* (London: Ebury Edge, 2023), p. 18.

to teach your subject is a key differentiator in effective teaching. It is at the core of what expertise means for a tutor.

Become competent and stay competent. It is so much easier than doubting yourself constantly.

Stop Making Excuses

I am embarrassed to share this next bit, but if it helps you, then it is worth it.

Every time I found tutoring hard, I made an excuse to get out of it. On those days when my self-doubt was too overwhelming, I found a way to let myself off the hook. Like a teenager bunking off to avoid a test or an employee chucking a sickie, I would decide that I wasn't feeling well and text to cancel before I could even stop myself. It was a weakness, a bad habit, and it really didn't look good to the parents.

Of course, we are all human and everyone gets ill occasionally, but schedules should mostly be set in stone. That way, both sides remain reliable and respectful. There are good reasons to change a schedule – but mine were not reasons, they were excuses. At the time, I couldn't begin to articulate what was really going on with me. I can now.

When I was a class teacher, I couldn't escape so easily. No matter how much I was dreading a new history or geography topic, there was no way out. When my self-doubt flared up and all I wanted to do was flee, I discovered that there are very few ways to escape teaching mid-year. I had to keep going.

I have learned that the process of pushing through can sometimes be enough to get me past my insecurities. I am a confident parent because of all the hours I have put in. I am quite a good cook because, whether I like it or not, the need to make dinner tends to come round daily.

But when you are working alone in your own home, it is too easy to make excuses and fail to show up as a professional.

Stop Treating Your Tutoring As Temporary

My husband, Simon, and I lived in four different rental properties during the first five years of our marriage. I was desperate to put down roots, to decorate and to make a house a home, but Simon kept reminding me that we wouldn't be staying there for long, so it didn't make sense to invest.

When we aren't ready to commit, we hold ourselves back. Whether you are tutoring thirty hours per week or three, unless you embrace your role as a tutor you will be holding back. As we have seen, the Plan B mindset serves no one.

In the case of the flat with chronic damp and blocked drains, it was logical to keep our bags by the door. But, with tutoring, every day that you don't embrace your role and responsibility as a professional tutor, you are letting down your students, and yourself.

Stop Thinking That Teachers Know Better

We know that tutoring can be more effective than classroom teaching. This is because of the tutor's ability to personalise the learning, dive deeply into detail and be more precise on pitch and pace, which we explore in depth in Part II.

A tutor can make learning more specific, planning a route based on where the student is starting from and where they need to get to. Make no mistake: teachers would love to work in this way. They would love to have plans based on a nuanced understanding of every student they teach. But they rarely have the time to build personal relationships, to assess effectively enough or to create follow-through on an individualised plan.

Once, when I was preparing for a school inspection, I naively asked my strongest teachers to give me 'evidence of differentiation – you know, three worksheets for top, middle and bottom'. Both teachers responded in the same way. They looked at me quizzically and said, 'There aren't three levels in our classes; there are thirty. Every student has a different blend of strengths and weaknesses. Every student is ready for a different next step and has to be supported in a unique way.'

Those were the strongest teachers in the school, and the task they set themselves was enormous. But what about everyone else? Every teacher who doesn't manage to develop such in-depth knowledge of each student, especially in secondary school where they see so many learners and so fleetingly?

Teachers who know their students well and build a deep understanding of what they know, what they can do and how they feel about their learning are rare in many secondary schools. Many teachers form broad judgements based on their experience of what a student will probably be able to do in the forthcoming lesson. It might be weeks before the teacher sees enough of their work to make any adjustments. Tutors can assess and adapt moment to moment. Teachers would love such a luxury.

There is a strong focus in the literature advising that the future of tutoring should comprise well-planned programmes designed by experienced teachers.[3] Yes, but also no. Close working relationships between the team around the child is ideal, but the assumption that the teacher knows better than the tutor is too school-centric. Tutors have the freedom to do things differently rather than providing more of the same. Let's not ruin that.

Moreover, well-planned programmes imply a lack of responsiveness. In Chapter 7, we will explore the power of assessment for learning. We will see that sticking to a planned programme risks undermining one of the three keys of effective tutoring – responsiveness.
The bottom line is that answers lie with the student, not with the

. . . .

3   Burtonshaw and Simons, *The Future of Tutoring*.

teacher. The more closely you read their cues, the more expert you will become.

Stop Doubting Your Efficacy

To really love tutoring you need to be able to enjoy the feeling of professional progress, and for this you need to measure how well your students are doing, all of which depends on being really clear about what you are trying to achieve. This is when I feel jealous of test prep tutors, as they know exactly what success looks like. With primary tutoring, the goals are looser and harder to pin down.

In Part II, we will explore how to measure your impact based on a clear understanding of what your goals are for each student. You will look at progress in outcomes and attitude. Aim to make this part of your routine. The more adept you can become at assessing your students' progress, the more confident you will become in your own effectiveness as a tutor.

Stop Waiting for the Bell to Ring

We are all survivors of school. We have been trained to raise our hand if we want to speak, to ask for permission to go to the bathroom, to start and stop work at the sound of a bell. It is a throwback to the factories of the Industrial Revolution. It is a system that habituates us to conform and comply, but it is no longer fit for purpose.

Having been in school for most of our lives, first as students and then as staff, many of us are used to living according to the calendars and timetables of the classroom. Like the adult elephant which has been tethered since it was a calf and doesn't realise that it now has the power to walk away, we underestimate ourselves. We need to recognise how transferrable our skills are, and we must learn to embrace stepping into the unknown.

This is not a book encouraging teachers to leave the classroom. That wouldn't be responsible, and nor is it necessary. The teachers who need to leave the profession are doing so already. They don't need encouragement, but they do need help.

There are now many coaches who specialise in guiding teachers into new employment. Some of these exiting teachers go into edtech, others go into the civil service or the third sector, and many turn to tutoring. It is an intuitive way for teachers to build on their years in the classroom and continue to do what they love. For these ex-teachers, tutoring may begin as a Plan B, but they must start to embrace it with intention. They must seek out the resources and support they need. They must learn to love tutoring.

We still need teachers in our classrooms, of course, but our students are not best served by teachers who feel trapped. As one school leader told me, 'Everyone's trying to escape the classroom: the children and the adults.' Hopefully, the teachers who remain will be the ones who truly want to be there and, by extension, they will create classrooms that children want to be in too.

Stop Thinking of Other Tutors As Your Competitors

When we compete with rather than support each other, we are reinforcing the old ideas of scarcity and compliance. There is no need for competition. When tutors are pitted against each other, no one wins. Other tutors are not your competitors; they are your colleagues. There is no lack of struggling students, unfortunately.

The best example I have seen of this in recent years has been on the NTP. During its launch, a certain number of companies were accepted on to the programme as Tuition Partners. Over the subsequent three years of delivering the programme, some of the leaders of these organisations have become a tight-knit group. As I have already mentioned, there were frequent challenges in the rollout of the NTP, and the Tuition Partners had to band together to support each other and advocate for themselves with the Department for Education. Ostensibly, these companies were competitors, vying for the same large school-based government-subsidised contracts, but, in reality, they shared a common experience and that created a shared bond and mutual respect. How cool is that?

Stop Answering to Parents

In an exclusive café in central London, over white tablecloths set with fine bone china, I had tea with a tutoring agency owner. To be honest, we didn't click. When I asked him what his 'why' was, he actually smirked. His was an old-school agency, composed mostly of retired teachers supporting upper-middle-class London-based families. He charged a premium for the postcode and took a hefty commission on every tutoring hour. Knowing all this, I shouldn't have been surprised to discover that he advises the parents to direct the tutor.

I don't tell my dentist how to fill my tooth or my lawyer how to draw up a contract. I choose the professionals I work with because I trust that they know their field better than I do, and I give them the space to do their job. Tutors deserve the same courtesy.

Tutors tend to have a much closer relationship with the parents than would be the case for a school teacher. In most cases, the parents are the client. Of course, there should be a strong line of communication between the tutor and the parents, and a shared understanding of where the student is up to and where they are headed. However, the power imbalance inherent in this agency leader's approach made me uncomfortable. I can only imagine how his tutors felt.

Although we are employed by parents and need to relate well to them, we must not be intimidated by them. Tutors are answerable to our own standards and code of conduct. This is the only way we can maintain our professional integrity. Whilst the parents may be paying the bill, our priority must be to serve the best interests of the student, even when that conflicts with the priorities of the parents.

Tutors take the role of the trusted adult very seriously. We know that all young people are potentially vulnerable and that we must be ready to advocate for them and their needs. Our aim is to support and enable our students, no matter what.

Parents can bring their own fear and baggage to the table, which can complicate things for the child. When this happens, we need to make a safe space for the student to learn what they need to, independent of the judgement of the parent.

One mother complained to me that she was running out of patience with her son who never understood his maths homework when she tried to help him. I politely insisted that the mother did no homework with her son whatsoever. I showed her that she was reinforcing his feeling of failure and that the best thing she could do was to leave it alone. The boy's anxiety was deeply rooted. By giving him a safe space to explore the foundations of number, I enabled him to rediscover maths without stress or embarrassment. He slowly built up his confidence as we worked together.

Parents are key stakeholders in the tutoring relationship, but they must give us the space to do our best work. We need their permission and their support, but we may also need them to keep their distance, so we can create the right environment for our students. We need to stop worrying about their opinions and remember that the student's needs are our main priority.

It is time to stop doubting, to stop fearing and to stop blaming. Our own limited thinking is often the source of our discomfort. So, let me assure you: parents and teachers don't have all the answers. Your position is a privilege and a responsibility. After all, the job you do has the power to improve lives, including your own.

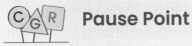 **Pause Point**

Which of the 'stop' statements here resonated with you the most?

. . . .

. . . .

What are the three things you worry about most as a tutor? What evidence do you have for each of them? What one thing could you do to improve on each of them?

. . . .

. . . .

What else could be holding you back? What can you do about it?

. . . .

. . . .

Love Tutoring Role Models:
Gospel Eadweardfilia

Gospel Eadweardfilia started tutoring in 2007 to pay off her student loan:

I'm the eldest, so I had to take care of the younger ones by myself. I had to know how to budget and everything else. Many people are quite surprised when I tell them I was living on £90 a month. But then I graduated, and the following year I got my student loan statement and it was more than I had planned. I was so shocked, I just burst out crying.

A friend suggested tutoring and, although a naturally shy person – 'The thought of going to speak to a stranger and teach a stranger terrified me' – she realised it was worth a try. She applied to a local agency and was offered some work. She soon found that tutoring improved her lifestyle:

I was still working in the pharmaceutical industry but tutoring as well to supplement my income. I paid off my student loan in about seven years. It should have taken me five years, but we like to travel and we like to eat in nice places.

Over the following decades, Gospel leaned into tutoring more and more:

I decided to structure my life in a way that I would do more tutoring and more tutoring online. I practise as a registered pharmacist two or three times a week, then the rest is tutoring, coaching and consulting.

Then Gospel started developing her skills in response to her students' needs:

> It has evolved over the years. I started exploring by adding financial literacy and also helping their parents. I'm certified as a mental health first-aider and financial coach. I'm a neuro-linguistic programmer practitioner and humanistic counsellor. I am also an emotional intelligence practitioner.

Gospel is in her element. 'I help, guide and inject hope in people.'

But she feels that the profession has changed since she started out in 2007:

> It's almost as if there are loads of people who have thought that this is a lucrative path to take, especially with the side hustle culture. So they just start up: 'Oh, I'm going to be tutoring.' But then they don't really put effort into it, and it's given tutoring a bad name.

Gospel lives with a long-term health condition, a genetic blood disorder, and says that online tutoring has kept her afloat:

> When I'm off work, I can tutor people. Tutoring has really saved me.

She adds:

> I want to champion those who have long-term health conditions to go into either tutoring or coaching, and have that as a first choice in their career, because I feel like it will reduce the amount of flare-ups and burnout they're going to go through.

What's next for Gospel? 'I don't want to do this all by myself. I want to clone myself!' Her dream is to train graduates of her financial literacy course to go into schools and run similar workshops on her behalf:

> *Tutoring has really opened doors for me too. I have done international speaking and all these other things. So, from that shy 20-something-year-old person, I am somebody who has her own company and is enjoying tutoring young people and seeing them achieve great things – isn't that fantastic?*

Gospel summed it up:

> *If you have tutoring as a first choice, it fits into your whole life. I can tutor anywhere in the world; I don't have to be in England. I have done that before. I'll just wake up one day and say, 'I need to get out of this place – it's doing my head in.' I take my laptop, I go to Dallas and I spend two weeks there. But I still tutor people and coach people, and then I come back refreshed!*

Part II

THE FOUNDATIONS OF EFFECTIVE TUTORING

State the Bloomin' Obvious

Now that we have explored why the Plan B mindset isn't the best way to think about your work as a tutor, we are ready to find out how to do things differently.

The material in this part is based on a course I wrote and have been delivering since 2019 for Qualified Tutor. The Foundations of Effective Tutoring course is designed to make evidence-based best practice in teaching relevant and accessible to tutors.

Creating material that is helpful for newbies and enriching for pros is always a challenge because every starting point is unique. My friend and former colleague, Adrian Conway, always advises me to 'state the bloomin' obvious'. But he has an unfair advantage: everything he says sounds profound when delivered in his laid-back Cumbrian lilt. I am a Londoner. I am guilty of both talking too fast and leaving too much unsaid. However, since this book is wholly in service of you and your progress, I am going to slow down and make things super clear.

I will do my best to model the effective teaching and learning we are aiming for in the pages that follow. I will present the biggest ideas in pedagogy using plenty of practical examples.

Throughout this book, you will find a series of original designs which I hope will make the abstract accessible. First, a caveat on conceptual models. They are a helpful way to organise and visualise complex ideas, and they create a mental hook on which to hang further information. I would encourage you to use them in your tutoring. However, for a model to be useful, it needs to be simple and memorable. Therefore, there will always be oversimplifications; no model is perfect.

Limitations notwithstanding, in giving tutoring its own conceptual models, informed by those of other professions, we build on the thinking that will take each of us – as individual tutors and as a global tutoring profession – to the next level.

Over the next five workshops we explore how you can become the tutor your student needs. Workshop 1 looks at professionalism in tutoring, which is the antidote to Plan B thinking. Workshop 2 is an overview of safeguarding and child protection. It will equip you to understand what child abuse is, and how you can do your part to protect your students. This workshop covers everything that schools include in staff training in England at the time of writing. Workshop 3 focuses on the relationship you will need to build with your student to optimise your sessions. This one will take some personal reflection on your part. Workshop 4 is the big teaching and learning piece. Using a model I created called 'The Learning Loop', you will learn what the best research-informed practice looks like and how to use an assessment-first approach to ensure you are always personalising the learning. Workshop 5 will cover the basics of special educational needs and mental health, and the mindset that will work best in working with these challenges.

As always, I have included pause points. Use them to take the learning and make it relevant to you. When you are curious, generous and reflective, the Foundations of Effective Tutoring course will transform your tutoring. As tutor Matthew Jones said, 'The content has definitely given me a lot of food for thought and has changed my behaviour and attitude to my own tuition in a short space of time. I am now listening to students more, making my sessions more engaging and giving more and more powerful feedback.'

Chapter 4

WORKSHOP 1: PROFESSIONALISM IN TUTORING

The 7Ps of Professionalism

Lying in bed reading a blog on my phone when I should have been getting the kids ready for school, I came across an apt word of Greek origin, *akrasia*, which means the state of mind in which someone acts against their better judgement through weakness of will. Oh, the irony.

However, if there has been a word for my self-defeating behaviour since the days of Ancient Greece, then I can be sure that I am not the only one. Let's say it even more clearly: I know that you already know that it is important to be professional. From your earliest days you have been reminded to be polite and punctual. But you also know that apples are better for you than chocolate biscuits. The fact is that we don't always behave in the ways we should.

People desperately want to **connect**, to **relate** and to **trust**.

The 7Ps of Professionalism is a model I devised to remind tutors what professional practice looks like. It is a model for real human beings – those of us who know how we should behave but don't always do so. I don't have a cure for akrasia (and, frankly, I am not sure I want one), but this chapter should give you some principles to raise up your practice from the inside out.

The professionalism I am pointing towards is warm and honest. It allows us to amplify all the things that make tutoring special. People desperately want to connect, to relate and to trust. It is no accident that my local bank branch has removed booths and queues and replaced them with sofas and dog biscuits. We no longer want distance and formality, even in our most trusted institutions. We want relatability, access and kindness. That has got to be our starting point.

The 7Ps of Professionalism is a set of values that can support us in staying safe and creating a safe environment for our students. It simultaneously creates boundaries and closeness. It allows us to be in control and to relax. It enables us to gain and maintain the respect of parents, students and schools. Crucially, it enables us to establish trust quickly and securely – and trust, as we shall see in the chapters that follow, is the catalyst for learning.

The 7Ps are preparedness, punctuality, politeness, presentability, positivity, patience and persistence. Taken separately they are all a good idea; taken together they create a powerful professional framework.

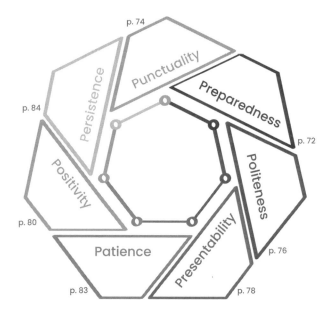

p. 74 Punctuality
p. 84 Persistence
Preparedness p. 72
Positivity p. 80
Politeness p. 76
Patience p. 83
Presentability p. 78

Let's unpick each of these 7Ps in the context of building ourselves into the tutors we want to be.

Preparedness

I was never outgoing enough to become a Girl Guide, and I don't write lists for fun (unlike many tutors I know), but I have learned over the years that preparation enables us to go beyond our natural limitations. Rather than avoiding positions of responsibility, I have learned to accept the need for preparedness.

In the context of tutoring, preparedness means a specific set of activities. It means planning, training and being ready to show up as a professional. It is the thinking and organising we do that sets us up for success.

Preparedness is about more than preparation, although it includes that crucial element. It is a state of mind. It is your life experience. It is the training you have done and the books you have read. Preparedness is your education and professional qualifications, your child protection and safeguarding training, and all the policies and procedures you follow as an independent tutor or when working with a tutoring business.

Many tutors feel that preparedness is make or break for them. We plan and replan a lesson, even though we know we might decide to do something completely different in the moment. We just feel so much more confident when we are organised. Planning for tutoring, as we will discuss in Chapter 6, can encompass a loose structure. You don't need a rigid plan because you need to be able to adapt as you go, although you will want something to use as a jumping-off point.

But preparation starts long before you meet your student. Training and professional development activities all fall within the category of preparedness. Every additional drop of learning should make you more ready to tutor well.

Thought experiments are a particularly effective way to prepare yourself for different eventualities. At Qualified Tutor, we like to take participants through scenarios during their tutor training. Thinking about planning, mental health or safeguarding in the context of a specific student makes it even more real. It also makes it more likely that if you were ever faced with a similar situation, you would feel that you had some prior experience to lean on. Some people like to do visualisations or manifestations to prepare themselves for all eventualities.

Rather than believing there is an authority just around the corner who is much more expert than you, it is time to step into that position yourself. All you need is to be willing to learn what is necessary to help those who are relying on you.

Pause Point

How prepared do you feel you currently are to tutor?

....

....

Notice what is good about your current preparation.

....

....

What could you do to become more prepared?

....

....

Punctuality

Why take the time to dwell on punctuality? Because it is the first impression you make and it gives all sorts of signals to your students. They may not notice if you are on time, but they will absolutely notice if you are late. We set out our stall in these initial moments by demonstrating that we are serious and that we intend to provide the best possible service.

Punctuality is also a perfect example of the power of reciprocity. The minute you are late, you signal to your student that it is alright for them to be late too. I speak with many tutoring businesses, especially those that employ undergraduate students, whose major bugbear is punctuality. It seems that far too many tutoring sessions, in person or online, start with stress because the tutor is late. Imagine how this feels for a student who is already vulnerable and hoping for your support. They may interpret your lateness as a lack of commitment, which will undermine the relationship you are working to build. Those few minutes can have lasting repercussions.

For me, punctuality also means finishing a session on time. We have all had meetings that have run on well beyond the expected time. This has two major results: you resent the speaker for not respecting your time and you are reluctant to attend their next meeting.

We are all human and mishaps happen, and that is okay. Your students need to know that you genuinely planned for punctuality; the rest is up to the universe.

Pause Point

What is your track record like for punctuality? What message do you think it is giving to your students?

....

....

If your answer to the above was less than ideal, can you spot any patterns in your behaviour? Which sessions do you tend to be late for? Do you struggle with a specific location or log-in? What happens in the hour preceding this session?

....

....

What practical strategies can you put in place to improve on your punctuality? What have you done in the past that might work here?

....

....

Politeness

No one likes to feel put on the spot, backed into a corner, or worse. Politeness, as interpreted by Brown and Levinson, is about 'saving face'.[1] The way we approach social interactions should be a factor in meeting our own needs and the needs of our students to feel safe and respected. Unfortunately, our culture is full of interactions that demoralise. As children, we are told what to do rather than being asked or invited. As adults, we are mocked and humiliated in the name of banter or sarcasm. You must do things differently and use politeness to create a safe space for your students.

There tends to be a lack of politeness where there is either an imbalance of authority or overfamiliarity. It is important that your student looks up to you as their leader in learning, and yet you must not be aloof or domineering. Equally, it is important that you and your students have a warm and trusting bond and yet keep a certain appropriate distance. Good manners help you to walk this path gracefully.

I learned in my role as a school leader that politeness is the best response to impoliteness. I don't mean cold civility; I mean genuine human decency. The kind that reminds us all that we are made of the same stuff. When we use politeness to show our students that we respect them, and that we respect ourselves by being consistent even when they challenge us, we show them that they are safe and we won't lash out at them.

I once used an online classroom to tutor a 10-year-old boy who struggled with maths anxiety. The platform has an excellent reporting function that generates a word cloud to let a teacher or parent know at a glance what was spoken about most frequently in a session. Usually, it will come up with key technical words such as 'osmosis' or 'Jane Austen' or 'football'. I was amused to discover that the word 'please' had been my most frequently used word in that session, which tells me that the student must have been behaving particularly badly!

....

1   P. Brown and S. Levinson, Universals in Language Usage: Politeness Phenomena. In E. N. Goody (ed.), *Questions and Politeness* (Cambridge: Cambridge University Press, 1978), pp. 56–289.

Pause Point

'Politeness is a less efficient but more effective mode of communication.' Do you agree?

....

....

Can you think of some examples when politeness has helped a student to save face?

....

....

How could you leverage the power of politeness more in your tutoring?

....

....

Presentability

There is a social etiquette for stepping into a home or school or onto a football pitch. Presentation is about cultural literacy. It is about appropriateness and signalling your alignment with the context in which you are working.

What do you look like when you turn up for work? What do your materials look like? You don't need to be in business attire and your worksheets don't need to be spiral bound, but you should dress for the environment you are stepping into and for the impression you want to create. There is no need to be overly formal; in most tutoring contexts, casual clothing is often more suitable.

Also keep in mind your commitment to child protection. There should be a required minimum standard of dress for you and your student to ensure an appropriate environment. Is it acceptable for your teenage student to open the door in his boxer shorts? Where you choose to draw this line is up to you, but you can be sure that your student will respect you for it.

When it comes to presenting your materials, be intentional about how you arrange your papers, your books and, if you are online, your video background. This means more than just tidying up or screening off your work area, although they could both be a good idea. Use your environment to communicate something about yourself, your values and interests. Think about the Year 1 teachers you know; they make their classroom walls work for them with posters and prompts. You can do the same.

When I ask you to think about your presentation, it isn't so that you can make things look perfect. It is so that you can be purposeful about how you appear and what you share. STEM tutor Georgina Green, who we met in Chapter 2, is excellent at getting her presentation just right. She knows her students appreciate her calm friendliness. Her video background reveals the most beautiful home. It is calm and serene, with a tidy kitchen and a fresh vase of flowers on the table behind her. When I am in a Zoom meeting with her, I always enjoy the tranquillity that her backdrop communicates. As Georgina says, 'It isn't about being something you are not. It's about showing the best of who you are.'

Don't forget social media. It is important to consider the way you present yourself on all your social media channels. Your student can easily look you up. Will you like what they see?

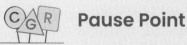 **Pause Point**

What do you think is the ideal presentation for your role? How do you think your presentation matches up to this?

....

....

Is there someone you could identify who does a great job of presenting themselves? What do you like about their presentation? How could you learn from it?

....

....

What improvements might you make to take your presentation to the next level?

....

....

Positivity

In their book, *How Full Is Your Bucket?*, Tom Rath and Donald Clifton report that '9 out of 10 people say they're more productive when they're around positive people'.[2] Using the metaphor of a bucket, the authors explain that we face a choice every moment of the day:

....

2   T. Rath and D. O. Clifton, *How Full Is Your Bucket? Positive Strategies for Work and Life* (New York: Gallup Press, 2004), p. 46.

to fill each other's buckets with positivity or to deplete them with negativity. Plus, and this is where it gets really powerful, whatever we choose to put into someone else's bucket is what we receive in our own. So, when we compliment a student's efforts, we feel good too. Conversely, if we come down heavy when they forget a book or arrive late, we are left feeling as bad as they do.

Well-being should be at the top of every curriculum. Our students need support with their confidence and sense of self as much as, if not more than, with their exams. The secret to positivity is simply: *look for the good*. Granted, it isn't easy to do if you aren't used to it, but this may be the single most important strategy in this book. Some days this will be easier than others, but if you train yourself to see the good rather than the bad, your student will thank you. 'Well done, Maya' is a far better behaviour management tool than, 'Hurry up, Maya', because, as Rath and Clifton say, positivity breeds productivity.

Rath and Clifton go further and actually give a 'magic ratio' for positive-to-negative interactions. They say that the optimal balance is five positive interactions to every one negative interaction, where neutral statements count on the negativity side. Any less positivity and the subject could suffer with stress, anger and hostility. But too much positivity can also be problematic, say Rath and Clifton. They state that ratios of above 13 to one, where the positives far outweigh the negative interactions, can feel false, becoming demotivating and eventually counterproductive. The power of positivity lies in its authenticity and its power to build your student's sense of self-worth. Use it wisely.[3]

It is amazing how powerful positivity can be to a disheartened student. It is the behaviour that will make them love us forever. Like most of the teachers I know, I have a drawer of thank-you notes from students over the years. When I left my recent post as a senior leader, the Year 6 children made me a 'Golden Book' because I was known for giving out gold stars for lovely work. Each girl wrote their own note, but the theme that runs through every single one is how much they appreciated my smile. One girl said, 'I remember in

. . . .
3   Rath and Clifton, *How Full Is Your Bucket?*, p. 57.

Year 4 I was very upset. You flashed me a smile and you made my day.' Of course, not everyone is smiley, and that's okay, but don't underestimate the power of a bright smile.

Whether you are tutoring online or in person, you can cultivate a positive environment and allow your students the space and time to adapt. In my case, think back to my bulging shelves, filled with books like *The Gruffalo* and *Elmer*. If you are online, consider using emojis, playing learning games or telling bad jokes. Anything to jump-start some good vibes. After all, a rising tide lifts all boats.

Pause Point

How do you think your students would rate you out of ten for positivity? How do you feel about that score?

....

....

Have you ever noticed the effect of your positivity on your students? What did you discover?

....

....

What can you do to bring more positivity into your tutoring persona?

....

....

Patience

Being patient with a student is one of the cornerstones of tutoring. Very few parents would send their child back to a tutor who had shouted at their child. Why would they?

I have been thinking a lot about patience recently, possibly because we are raising a Labrador puppy. Our black Lab Moxie is now five months old. She is adorable and an absolute handful. Much like a toddler, she needs love and attention, she needs management and guidance, and she needs us to factor her in constantly. I am a patient person, but she has found my limits once or twice – usually, in the morning when she nabs the just-packed lunches off the kitchen counter!

Moxie is an unbridled creature of impulse; she is motivated by satisfying her desires. When I ask her to sit and wait for a treat, I can feel the tension in her. She wants to leap *and* she wants to stay. She is learning to self-regulate.

Claire Cant is a passionate tutor of mathematics. She loves to present her students with puzzles and problems, although she admitted to me that she struggles to be patient whilst she waits for her students to find a solution which, to her, is jumping off the page. Then she came up with a wonderful strategy: every time she finds herself wondering why they find it so difficult, she imagines trying to juggle. 'I don't find maths hard,' she told me, 'but I'm not very good at juggling, yet.' Claire said that putting herself in the shoes of a novice, albeit in a different domain, has helped her to be patient whilst her students take the time they need to get there.

Studies show that giving just three seconds of thinking time improves outcomes, but most teachers wait for an average of just 0.9 seconds between asking a question and speaking again themselves.[4] It is understandable, since they are under so much pressure to keep up the pace and hold the attention of the class, but when we are working one-to-one or in small groups there really is

---

4   M. B. Rowe, Wait Time: Slowing Down May Be a Way of Speeding Up! *Journal of Teacher Education*, 37(1) (1986), 43–50 at 44.

no rush. If we want our students to think deeply, we must give them the time and space they need to do so.

Pause Point

'Patience is make or break.' Do you agree with this statement? What are your thoughts on the subject?

....

....

We all struggle with patience sometimes. Take a moment to acknowledge your triggers without judgement.

....

....

Knowing what tests your patience, how can you plan your tutoring to mitigate for those moments?

....

....

Persistence

What do you do if your students don't understand an explanation you have given? You try another one, of course. And then another one after that. The best tutors I know are constantly looking for new ways to explain ideas. They have a wide range of tools available to them in the tutoring toolbox, so they can always find a way through. This persistence means the world to a student.

Persistence makes you trustworthy to your student and to yourself. It is built on a growth mindset, building a track record of courage, commitment and a willingness to go above and beyond. For me, persistence is the key to everything, although it is also the one I find hardest from the 7Ps.

What do you do when the going gets tough? It is fine to feel stuck, to be stumped, to want to go back to bed with a packet of biscuits and a mug of hot tea. As long as you don't – or, at least, not for too long.

CGR Pause Point

What makes you feel stuck or ready to give up?

. . . .

. . . .

When have you managed to make it past those tricky moments and felt proud of your subsequent accomplishments?

. . . .

. . . .

How can you build accountability and encouragement into your day so you can continue to be persistent?

. . . .

. . . .

Chapter 5

WORKSHOP 2: SAFEGUARDING FOR TUTORS

What scares you most about tutoring? For me, it is an allegation of misconduct. The thought of being accused of wrongdoing makes me want to curl up into a ball and hide under my duvet. I don't mind making mistakes or saying something stupid, but the idea of putting myself or my students in harm's way causes a powerful physiological response. Even as I write this, my teeth are clenched and my heart is racing. I don't feel safe.

I know more than one teacher whose life has been ruined by an allegation of misconduct which has subsequently proven to be false. Reputations are fragile. When I let myself think about this, I wonder whether maybe it really is too much – and, again, I am back under the duvet in my mind.

This was the hardest part of this book to write for two reasons – one is emotional and one practical.

Exploring the ways in which children are harmed is emotionally disturbing. For those of us who prefer to dwell in positive and gentle spaces, confronting such harsh realities can be shocking, but it is our duty. This extract from the UK's statutory guidance for schools and colleges explains why: 'If children and families are to receive the right help at the right time, *everyone* who comes into contact with them has a role to play in identifying concerns, sharing information and taking prompt action.'¹ Tutors have a role to play in keeping children safe too. Therefore, no matter how uncomfortable the topic of child abuse might feel, we must address it.

However, just as we are committed to looking after our young people, we also have a responsibility to look after ourselves and each other. When I deliver this training, I remind participants to be mindful of their own feelings and those of other participants in the group. As we move through this chapter, be gentle with yourself. If you feel you need to reach out for professional support, please don't hesitate to do so. You are as precious as any of our students.

The second reason for this section being tricky to write is that certain aspects are specific to time and place. Today, England, Wales, Scotland and Northern Ireland all have policies for safeguarding and child protection. We have learned from the tragic mistakes of earlier generations. The education community is well-rehearsed on how to respond to safeguarding concerns. We aim to be vigilant.

Policies may be different in other countries, but the principles and the commitment to the well-being of our children remains the same. For those of you who are not in the UK or are working with students abroad, please be proactive and find out what the right resources are for safeguarding in your context.

---

1   Department for Education, *Keeping Children Safe in Education 2023: Statutory Guidance for Schools and Colleges. Part One: Information for All School and College Staff* (1 September 2023), p. 4 (original emphasis). Available at: https://www.gov.uk/government/publications/keeping-children-safe-in-education--2.

'If children and families are to receive **the right help at the right time**, *everyone* who comes into contact with them has **a role to play** in identifying concerns, sharing information and taking prompt action.'

Recognise, Respond, Report

The recognise, respond, report model can help to guide the process of supporting young people, although it needs to be handled with care. Child protection is full of grey areas: for every one clear-cut case, there will be hundreds of complex, nuanced and 'it depends' situations. The bottom line is always to take things seriously. The risk of ridicule for reporting something innocent is nothing compared to the risk of ignoring a genuine case of abuse.

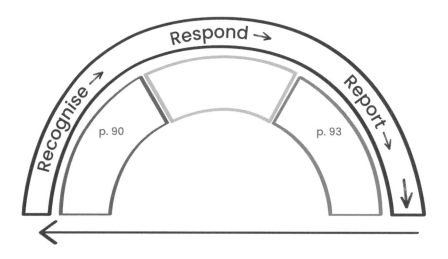

Recognise

At Qualified Tutor, we always start our safeguarding training with learning what to look out for. Knowing the following definitions of abuse, and how prevalent the different types are, will help you to pay attention to the welfare of your students. You should always be alert for changes in behaviour. The better your knowledge of and relationship with your student, the more likely you are to recognise any causes for concern.

Let's look at some definitions and statistics for the main categories of abuse identified by the UK's primary source of safeguarding support, training and data, the NSPCC.

- **Sexual abuse** involves a child or young person being 'forced, tricked or manipulated into sexual activities'.[2] An estimated '1 in 20 children in the UK have been sexually abused' – the vast majority by someone they know.[3]

- **Physical abuse** is defined as 'deliberately hurting a child and causing physical harm'. Around '1 in 14 children in the UK have been physically abused'.[4]

- **Emotional abuse** is the 'emotional maltreatment of a child, which has a severe and persistent negative effect on the child's emotional development. It's also known as psychological abuse. Most forms of abuse include an emotional element, but emotional abuse can also happen on its own.' The NSPCC report that 'Around 1 in 15 children in the UK have been emotionally abused by a parent or carer.' Most child abuse also includes an element of emotional abuse.[5]

- **Neglect** is 'not meeting a child's basic physical and psychological needs. It is a form of child abuse that can have serious and long-lasting impacts on a child's life – it can cause serious harm and even death.' It is the most common form of abuse. Around '1 in 10 children in the UK have been neglected'.[6]

- **Radicalisation** is 'the process through which a person comes to support or be involved in extremist ideologies. It can result in

---

2   See https://www.nspcc.org.uk/what-is-child-abuse/types-of-abuse/child-sexual-abuse.

3   National Society for the Prevention of Cruelty to Children, *Statistics Briefing: Child Sexual Abuse* (March 2021), pp. 1, 12. Available at: https://learning.nspcc.org.uk/media/1710/statistics-briefing-child-sexual-abuse.pdf.

4   National Society for the Prevention of Cruelty to Children, *Statistics Briefing: Physical Abuse* (September 2021), pp. 2, 3. Available at: https://learning.nspcc.org.uk/media/2669/statistics-briefing-physical-abuse.pdf.

5   National Society for the Prevention of Cruelty to Children, *Statistics Briefing: Emotional Abuse* (December 2021), pp. 3, 6. Available at: https://learning.nspcc.org.uk/media/2717/statistics-briefing-emotional-abuse.pdf.

6   National Society for the Prevention of Cruelty to Children, *Statistics Briefing: Neglect* (July 2021), pp. 2, 3. Available at: https://learning.nspcc.org.uk/media/2621/statistics-briefing-neglect.pdf.

a person becoming drawn into terrorism and is in itself a form of harm.'[7]

- **Drug trafficking/county lines** is 'a form of criminal exploitation where urban gangs persuade, coerce or force children and young people to store drugs and money and/or transport them to suburban areas, market towns and coastal towns ... It can happen in any part of the UK and is against the law and a form of child abuse.'[8]

- **Female genital mutilation (FGM)** is 'the partial or total removal of the external female genitalia for non-medical reasons. It's also known as female circumcision or cutting.'[9]

How you respond to a safeguarding concern can make an enormous difference to the well-being of a child. In the first instance, clearly note down the facts as you recognise them, whether it is bruising, a change in behaviour, fearfulness or inappropriate sexualised behaviour. Date your records and keep them in a safe place.

Three Don'ts of Disclosure

It takes immense bravery for a child to make a disclosure and let someone know they are being abused: 'They might be worried about the consequences or that nobody will believe them. They might've told someone before and nothing was done to help them. Sometimes they might not know what's happening to them is abuse and struggle to share what they're feeling.'[10] Some children might put up with abuse for months or even years, and some may never tell anyone.

---

7   See https://learning.nspcc.org.uk/safeguarding-child-protection/radicalisation.
8   See https://learning.nspcc.org.uk/child-abuse-and-neglect/county-lines.
9   See https://learning.nspcc.org.uk/child-abuse-and-neglect/fgm.
10 See https://www.nspcc.org.uk/keeping-children-safe/reporting-abuse/what-to-do-child-reveals-abuse.

If a student does make a disclosure to you, there are a few rules that you must follow:

1   Don't ask leading questions. A student who is eager to please could easily be misled into saying something untrue because they thought it was the right thing to say.

2   Don't express disbelief as it could cause the child to retreat back into silence.

3   Don't promise confidentiality because you will need to involve the appropriate professionals to ensure that a child is removed from an abusive situation.

Report

If in doubt, report. Your report might be the event that finally gets a child out of harm's way, or it could be one more piece of evidence in a long line of concerns. If it turns out to be nothing at all, well, that is great news. No one sensible will ever resent you taking a child's safety seriously, no matter how painful or embarrassing it might feel.

By intervening early, some family situations can be improved before they escalate. Support such as home visits, benefits and counselling can be put into place to protect and improve outcomes for the child – which is another reason not to hesitate.

How and where to report will depend on your student's location. It can be tricky to know whether to speak with the student's parents – after all, they could be the abusers. Tutors working for an agency will be expected to report to their designated safeguarding lead (DSL). Tutors working independently tend to rely on the DSL in the student's school. For this reason, it can be helpful to get the name of the student's school as part of your onboarding process, which takes me to the final topic we need to cover under safeguarding and child protection.

If you are taking on other tutors to work for you or alongside you, you must have a safer recruitment policy in place. This means taking steps to ensure that you employ only those individuals who are suitable for working with young people: 'Safer Recruitment is a vital part of creating a safe and positive environment and making a commitment to keep children safe from harm.'[11] By making it clear to applicants from the outset that your tutoring organisation requires police record checks, independent references, interviews, CVs and application forms, you are putting up an immediate deterrent to predators.

Of course, expectations differ in some instances. For example, a tutor organisation that works with young people at risk of criminal activities may not consider a clear police record a necessary requirement for tutors. In fact, they might find that adults who have had similar experiences are more relatable and therefore more helpful to the students. Context is key: we need to be aware of the needs of our students at all times.

Finally, you must always assess the risk to yourself in any situation. If you don't feel safe in a session, you must remove yourself immediately and report it to a DSL or the police.

11 See https://learning.nspcc.org.uk/safeguarding-child-protection/safer-recruitment.

Pause Point

Find out what the regulation is where you live. Look up the relevant safeguarding policy and ensure that you know what to look out for and how to report.

. . . .

. . . .

Think about how you work currently. Where do you make notes? To whom would you report a concern? To whom would you direct any questions about safeguarding?

. . . .

. . . .

Now that you understand what it means to keep yourself safe and keep children safe in education, I would love to know how the role makes you feel. Most of us feel a mixture of privilege and overwhelm, and that is okay. How do you feel about being the trusted adult for your student?

. . . .

. . . .

I have come to a frightening conclusion.

I am the decisive element in the classroom.

It is my personal approach that creates the climate.

It is my daily mood that makes the weather.

As a teacher I possess tremendous power to make a child's life miserable or joyous.

I can be a tool of torture or an instrument of inspiration.

I can humiliate or humor, hurt or heal.

In all situations it is my response that decides whether a crisis will be escalated or de-escalated, and a child humanized or de-humanized.[1]

1   H. G. Ginott, *Teacher and Child: A Book for Parents and Teachers* (New York: Macmillan, 1972), p. 15.

Chapter 6

WORKSHOP 3: RELATIONSHIP MATTERS

Tutoring is a highly relational discipline. Relationship is the first key to effective tutoring and the subject of this chapter. It is the conduit for learning. It doesn't take much time to establish a good tutoring relationship, and it will accelerate the progress your student makes. Taking the time to get to know your student and to check in with them at the beginning of every lesson can help you get to know each other, and tailor each session effectively.

I am going to outline some guidelines based on the three qualities of a great tutoring relationship: positivity, respect and trust. But, first, let's take a moment with this much-loved quote on page 96 from psychologist Haim Ginott's book, *Teacher and Child*.

We must take responsibility for creating the right atmosphere for learning. Realise the power you hold to make a real difference to your student. Seize the opportunity and make the most of it.

If you hear yourself complaining that your student wasn't in the mood today, that they don't seem interested or that they don't do the prep, remember this quote and accept it as an invitation to improve something about yourself rather than trying to fix the student. Ask yourself: how can I modify the climate in my sessions so that it all becomes more joyous?

Creating a Culture of Learning

A great deal of what effective tutors do is cultivating a healthy learning culture. Even if you have never heard this phrase, which comes from the science of organisational processes, you will have first-hand experience of it. Consider who you loved to learn from as a child. A grandparent? A head teacher? A football coach? What did these people bring to their learning culture? Maybe commitment, curiosity or challenge? A sense that learning is the best thing in the world? That is what your students need you to create for them.

My friends, Nicola and Matt Tiller, have home-educated all three of their sons. Far from being lonely, the children meet up with a broad group of home-ed families and are better socialised than most of the children I know. They have an amazing schedule of activities that includes swimming, acting and weekends at circus camp. Nicola will stop in the street to explain drainage, photosynthesis or reproduction. She illustrates complex ideas in a way that her children can access because they are perfectly attuned to one another.

I can't assure you that their 9-year-old's reading is ahead of my 8-year-old's, but why should it be? He is a different child, with different strengths, raised in a different learning culture. The education they are providing for their children is stimulating, diverse and enriching. It is exciting to witness.

What is amazing about Nicola and Matt's family is how much effort they all put in, the children as well as the adults. In theory, it would be much easier for everyone if the boys went to school like every other child in the neighbourhood. But what Nicola and Matt have done by opting out of mainstream schooling is to pursue their own learning culture – one based on curiosity and adventure. I am not advocating for home education here, as I don't understand it well enough yet, but I am encouraging an approach to learning that is immersive and meaningful.

How would you define your learning culture? Are you a no-nonsense languages specialist or a wacky maths nerd? Are you a flowery English expert or a high-energy, fast-talking 11+ group tutor?

Remember my bookcases with *Elmer* and *The Gruffalo*? Remember the biscuits and juice? I am all about 'learning can be lovely'. What are you about? Don't worry about looking silly. Tap into your own love of learning and find a way to share that with your students.

 Pause Point

Describe your favourite learning experience. What three words would sum up that memory for you?

· ·

· ·

Think about your own learning environment. What three words would your students use to describe working with you as a tutor?

· ·

· ·

Is there alignment between those two descriptions? What could you do to really create the learning environment you dream of?

· ·

· ·

Start with Why

Understandably, your student is both hopeful and mistrustful of you as their tutor. You are not the first adult who has promised to make the difficult easy or the unimaginable possible, to turn 'I can't' into 'I can'.

If you have been engaged by the parents, there is probably a story to uncover. There may be a long stream of small or large disappointments. Your student is probably afraid: afraid of failing you, afraid of failing their parents, afraid of failing themselves, afraid of failing at life. They will want to believe that this time it will stick and the sun will shine once more. But they just don't dare.[1]

Being proactive and creating clear and consistent messaging about who you are and what you are all about will allow you to build rapport and, more gradually, trust. Ask yourself: Why should they trust you? Why will it be different this time?

Simon Sinek, the author of *Find Your Why*, says: 'people don't buy what you do; people buy Why you do it'.[2] If a student comes to you disenchanted and ready to give up on themselves, you really need them to buy into your Why. You need them to believe that you care. You need them to believe that they can improve. Without that agreement, it is going to be impossible to help them.

So, you are going to have to answer this important question: Why do you tutor? Is it just to make money, or is there more to it than that? It is true that tutoring is more convenient than bar work and more stimulating than data entry, but if you don't have a deeper motivation, your student will struggle to trust you.

In the Qualified Tutor community, one of our onboarding questions is, 'What is your Why?' Of course, some people find this question

---

1   If you think this sounds overdramatic, then you are underestimating the powerful messages children get from our high-stakes education system.
2   S. Sinek, How Great Leaders Inspire Action, *TED.com* [video] (September 2009). Available at: https://www.ted.com/talks/simon_sinek_how_great_leaders_inspire_action. See also S. Sinek with D. Mead and P. Docker, *Find Your Why: A Practical Guide for Discovering Purpose for You and Your Team* (New York: Portfolio/Penguin, 2017).

easier than others. It can take a while to go deep, but when they do it transforms their mindset. Having read thousands of inspiring responses to this question, I have learned that the motivation to tutor falls into four broad categories:

1   To support struggling learners.

2   To instil a love of a subject.

3   To inspire as they were inspired.

4   To give others what they wish they had received.

Which of these answers resonates with you? Are you the special needs tutor who wants their student to have the advocate they never had? Are you the science tutor who wants to inspire female students to go into STEM professions? There is no right answer here; it is simply about honest reflection.

Finding your own Why is only half the story. The other half is understanding your student's motivations. Do they need a 7 in GCSE biology so they can do an A level because they dream of becoming a psychotherapist? Do they need to smash their 11+ because there is a certain private school with a swimming pool they are desperate to attend? Do they need to pass functional maths and English so they can get onto an apprenticeship?

Notice that we are talking about the Why of the student, not the motivation of the parents, which can be more complex and problematic. It doesn't serve anyone if children become stressed and anxious to perform, and it often reveals a misalignment in the various Whys of the various stakeholders: a parent wanting their child to get top grades to impress their community or a school pushing the child to excel because they need to maintain their position in the league tables. These motivations are rife within education, but they are not our concern as tutors.

If we concentrate on working out what motivates our student (e.g. feeling less foolish in a maths lesson) and what motivates us (e.g. developing their confidence in maths), then we can build the tutoring relationship on solid foundations and really make an impact. When you find your motivation, and understand how it aligns with the needs of your students, you will create a meaningful shared purpose between yourself and your learner.

One tutor who is redefining tutoring today is Claire Smith, who has an award for her achievements as head of education in prisons across the UK. Working with Nudge Education, which offers government-funded therapeutic interventions on a one-to-one basis for our most chronically disengaged young people, Claire helps her students to improve their opportunities with vocational training and functional skills. She brings all her life experience to the table and tells her young students straight: if you continue like this, you will end up in prison. Claire isn't afraid of tough truths, and is in high demand at Nudge because her students trust her. She is giving them opportunities, igniting hope and preparing them for a better life.

Your Why doesn't have to be as grand as Claire's. It could simply be, as it was for me, wanting to give students a feel for how lovely learning can be. Thinking back to my own childhood, my memories are like something from a Roald Dahl book. I learned that learning can be lovely in preschool, with teachers who could be compared to *Matilda*'s Miss Honey, all soft innocence, whilst the middle and senior years turned distinctly Trunchbull, with adults who didn't seem to like children much.

Thus, I became a primary tutor who used Miss Honey as a model for making Matildas. It may sound trite, but if we aren't honest then what are we? That was my motivation, and that was what I was employed to do. Parents who wanted their child to have a gentler educational experience would give their children the gift of my time. Together, we built confidence and enjoyment, which created a touchstone that hopefully will stay with them for life.

What is your Why? What is the learning culture you are looking to foster? Once you have really dug into your motivations, and the values and beliefs that underpin them, you will become more able to communicate them to your student. The warm smile, the superhuman patience, the framed pictures of women in science – all these cues come together to signal where you are coming from and to invite the student along.

Think again about the adult who inspired you to learn from the previous task on creating a learning culture. How did you know they were in it for the right reasons? Did they tell you? Or did they show you through their behaviours and the way they showed up for you?

The 7Ps of Professionalism in Chapter 4 is a good tool for you here. Your student will know that you care about them and their needs by how prepared, punctual, polite, presentable, positive, patient and persistent you are. That is how they will learn what is important to you.

You may also choose to recount your own story to them, so they have a context for your commitment. When you tell them about your own struggles with dyslexia, and how it eventually became your superpower, you will put them at ease and help them to feel aligned with you. Telling your story is one of the best things you can do for your students. They want to build a relationship with you, and to do that they need to understand you, so, if possible, try to tell them a bit about your background and how it inspired you to be the tutor you are today.

Once you can convey in words and action your commitment to the student and the subject, you need to go to where your student is. Empathise and align. A student who struggles with quadratic equations needs you to feel the fear before you can help them. A student who can't swim needs you to stay in the shallow end and just float. However, this is just the beginning. It isn't enough to reassure; we also need to help.

Pause Point

What is your Why as a tutor?

....

....

What are some of your students' Whys?

....

....

How well do they align? How well do you feel you communicate
your Why to your students? How could you do so more clearly?

....

....

The Three Steps to a Productive Tutoring Relationship

Building a relationship is a step-by-step process. The first step is
positivity, the second is respect and the third is trust. Trust is our
ultimate goal when establishing a productive tutoring relationship,
but it takes time. Each of these stages is built on the one before:
respect builds on positivity and trust builds on respect. You can't
skip a step but, if necessary, you can go back and reinforce an
earlier stage.

The Three Building Blocks

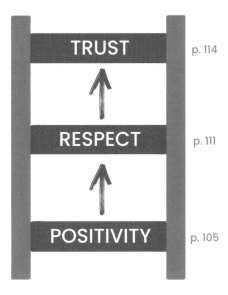

Step 1: Positivity

We have already explored the importance of being positive for our students, but let's think about it from the student's perspective. Most tutors enjoy a warm relationship with their students; we pride ourselves on building a comfortable rapport. We start each session with a friendly smile and a quick chat. We cheer their wins and we lean in with support when they are having a tough time. We give our students a sense that we are there for them.

Happy Children Learn

Whether you are tutoring online or in person, positivity is an incredibly powerful tool, and it isn't difficult to create. If you can cultivate a positive environment for your students, you have a chance of returning them to a natural state of curiosity and play, which are the foundations for learning.

Babies and young children naturally absorb information, develop skills and make connections. As they grow up and become affected by the world around them, this openness to learning usually diminishes. If there is one thing we want to do as educators, it is to reclaim that openness for our students and ourselves.

Unfortunately, most children learn at some point during the first ten years of life that it isn't worth having a go. That it is safer to stay on the sidelines than to get stuck in. That it just isn't worth the risk. Compliance replaces creativity and learning slows.

This fear of judgement stays with many of us for our entire lives. It is what holds us down, holds us back and holds us hostage to our own inner critic. How much more art, music and literature would there be if we had never been told to stop playing and start studying? How much happier would we all be if we still understood that play is the best learning and that the best learning feels like play?

There is a wealth of research on the effects of happiness on learning. Studies show that happiness improves memory (dopamine and serotonin are associated with the brain's ability to make connections), that there is a 'reciprocal causality' between happiness and learning, and that anxiety and depression can have a negative effect on academic achievement.[3]

In other words, if you are happy, then you will learn well; and if you learn well, then you will become happier.

Be Friendly and Be Fun

We need to help our students achieve this kind of virtuous cycle, so their happiness and their achievements can grow together. It isn't complicated. You need to be two things: friendly and fun.

At the start of a session, treat your student to a warm welcome and ask them how they are doing. Taking the time to build rapport and get in tune with your student will help the rest of the session go smoothly. It will enable you to get to know them and help them to

. . . .

3   P. D. Quinn and A. L. Duckworth, Happiness and Academic Achievement: Evidence for Reciprocal Causality. Paper presented at the Annual Meeting of the American Psychological Society, Washington, DC, 24–27 May 2007.

How much happier would we all be if we still understood that **play is the best learning** and that **the best learning feels like play**?

feel cared for. Rather than sweeping to the side whatever is going on in their lives, give them a moment to share what they need to, so you can tailor the session even more effectively. Remember to keep the tone pleasant and upbeat. Be supportive and celebrate their successes. It can seem obvious to say 'be friendly', but as adults we get stuck in our own heads so easily that a reminder that dedicating some time to making your student feel seen and accepted is probably not wasted words.

Unlike their class teacher, your student isn't tied to you. If they really want to, they can walk away. You don't want them to do that, of course, because you want them to stay with you long enough for you to help them.

The peak—end rule is a theory which states that we only remember the peaks and the end of any event. Simply by creating two fun moments in your sessions, you keep your student eager to come back for more. You don't have to create balloon animals in every session, just try to structure your activities so they aren't too dry – spice them up with a story, a game or a challenge. (Yes, even if you are teaching A level physics!)

Surprises, Not Prizes

It is worth exploring the distinction between intrinsic and extrinsic motivation here.

Intrinsic motivation is the inner yearning to make progress for its own sake. This is the goal – we all want our students to love learning. When someone has intrinsic motivation, they develop two vital skills: metacognition (the ability to notice our own learning processes) and self-regulation (to keep that process on track). When we develop these two skills, we have the power of self-determination. We can direct our own learning.

In contrast, extrinsic motivation is carrots and sticks – or, in our case, maybe crisps and stickers – which is what education and Western society tends to run on. Points, praise and, eventually, years later, performance-related pay and end-of-year bonuses are deployed from our earliest days to keep us on task. In the learning context, the problem with extrinsic motivation is that not only does it distract us from the learning, but we also struggle to develop the key skills of self-regulation and metacognition. With the promise of a treat or the threat of failure looming over us, we literally can't hear ourselves think.

But how do we move students from extrinsic to intrinsic motivation? This is one of the biggest and juiciest problems in education today.

Most children are so habituated to the sticker chart methodology that they flounder without it. You may need to use rewards simply to keep their attention. That's fine, but at the same time try to redirect them towards something more meaningful. Replace toys and treats with stories and games. Give them Lego blocks and let them build a tower or sing a silly celebration song when they achieve something important.

Over time, try to help your students to notice the beauty of learning and the feeling of making progress for its own sake. Use language like 'Look what you can do!' and 'Isn't that fascinating?' to direct their focus towards the learning. With consistent effort, you can ween them off extrinsic motivation.

Toxic Praise

Praise is a complicated art, and the wrong type of praise can be like salt water to a thirsty person. We must avoid making the students' value conditional on their achievements.

Praising a student's personality or characteristics, rather than their work, can make them feel dependent and therefore vulnerable. Praising a student in relation to someone else can make them competitive and insecure. Praising a student excessively can make them doubt your authenticity.

Therefore, praise a student for their efforts rather than their achievements. Praise them for what is within their control. Praise them in a way that shows them how to praise themselves.

It is worth remembering these important points about toxic praise. This is a call for you to think deeply about the power of your words. It is an opportunity to reflect on your learning culture and your why, and to use praise intentionally to build up your student.

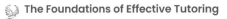

If this all seems too abstract, this is basically what you need to know: praise the effort, not the person. Rather than 'Good girl' say 'Great work!' Instead of 'You're so clever' say 'That was clever!' If you separate the learning from the learner, you can't go far wrong.

Pause Point

How comfortable are you being friendly and fun?

....

....

Plan a fun five-minute activity that will leave your student eager and excited to learn with you.

....

....

How did that feel? Were you confident or out of your comfort zone? How can you integrate more fun into your tutoring?

....

....

Step 2: Respect

In addition to creating a positive relationship, my students also need me to create a respectful one. I must have boundaries, set high expectations and establish a safe space to help them make the most of each session.

Whilst behavioural issues are lessened in one-to-one and small group tutoring, in comparison to whole-class teaching, they can still arise. It always helps to have some strategies in place to maintain a calm and conducive learning environment. By creating an atmosphere of mutual respect, you can ensure that your sessions run smoothly and with minimal disruption.

Respect in tutoring comes from two places: the respect we all owe to each other and the respect born of a shared purpose. Your student should respect you because you are inherently worthy of respect, and you should respect your student because they are too.

Plus, you and your student are on a learning journey together; neither of you will get there without the other's help. Think of J. K. Rowling's fictional characters Harry Potter and Professor Dumbledore. It is only together that they can defeat the evil Voldemort and save the wizarding world.

All Behaviour is Communication

If you find that your student is struggling to show you appropriate respect, think about Haim Ginott's quote at the beginning of this chapter about the teacher's mood creating the weather. How could you prepare better for these sessions? How could you design your time together to better suit your student's needs? Could you swap the day or time? Could you change the room or go outside? Is the work too hard or too easy? Could you make it feel more relevant? Consider the needs of the student and what they might be responding to – or, better still, ask them and show how much you care.

Of course, as the trusted adult, it is important not to take anything too personally, but, equally, it isn't helpful to let your student trample on your feelings. In fact, pushing back can be a constructive reaction. As young people find their feet they need a safe adult to push against. The 11-year-old daughter of a close friend of mine, who was once quite rude to me when I picked her up from school, was completely shocked when I pulled her aside and quietly explained that she might not realise it, but I genuinely cared what she thought. From the look on her face, she had forgotten that I was a person too. Let's be honest: this is something we have all done when tired and hungry or swept up in a bad mood. Or, as one very experienced mum I know put it, 'After a long day at school, they've just run out of good behaviour.'

If your student continues to behave with disrespect, treat respect as a learning objective and teach it the way you would any other skill. Be patient and persistent and you will get there.

Having said all of this, your red lines should be clear. You need to know what is and isn't acceptable for you, and you need to be consistent. I would recommend setting some ground rules at the beginning of any new tutoring relationship. As a teacher, I used to create a class contract or a code of conduct. Tutors don't need anything quite so formal, but it is helpful to take a moment early on to agree on how you are going to work together. Talk about how each of you would like the tutoring to be and then follow through.

The nice thing about this conversation is that it works with any age group, from toddler to adult learner. Simply describe what you like and don't like to happen when you tutor, and ask your student to do the same. For instance, I might say to a student:

> 'You don't need to call me Mrs Silver, Julia is just fine.'

> 'Even if you aren't sure, I want you to have a go.'

> 'Please don't be shy. Ask me your questions – I'm here to help.'

They might say:

> 'I don't like to be rushed.'

> 'I prefer to use the chat [function] than to speak in a group.'

'I like to work in coloured pens because in school we're only allowed pencils.'

These things sound simple but they can create an atmosphere of mutual respect. Simply by reminding your student that you are keeping to your side of the deal, you can encourage them to keep to theirs: 'I'm being careful not to rush you. Are you making sure you're having a go, even if you aren't sure you'll get it right?'

 Pause Point

List your non-negotiables. What do you expect from your student in terms of respectful behaviour?

....

....

What can your student expect from you? If you like, you can list these in two columns: rights (what we have a right to expect) and responsibilities (what can rightfully be expected of us).

....

....

Aim to write out these lists twice, once from your own point of view and once from the point of view of your student.

....

....

Step 3: Trust

Trust helps us to get the job and it also helps us to keep the job. We need parents to trust us with their children, with their time and with their money. The 7Ps of Professionalism will help with this, but that is just the beginning. We also need the students to trust us. They need to trust that our goals are aligned with theirs, that we will be steadfast in our commitment to them, and that we can and will help them to get where they need to go. Finally, we need to help our students to learn to trust themselves.

But trust is precious and fragile, and it isn't given easily, especially by the students that tend to need a tutor. If they have struggled in the classroom, if they have been disappointed and become disheartened, they will probably be cautious about giving their trust.

Every time I cancelled a session, arrived insufficiently prepared or failed to follow through on something I had promised a student, I undermined my own trustworthiness. I caused them to doubt me and my intentions. I failed to give them the sense of rock-solid security they needed from me. This wasn't a failure in planning; it was a failure in trustworthiness. It was classic Plan B mindset. My students deserved so much more.

The theory of relational trust was developed by researchers Anthony Bryk and Barbara Schneider, who describe the importance of four considerations for trustful relationships in educational settings: respect, personal regard, competence in core responsibilities and personal integrity.[4] Far from a Plan B mindset, this is commitment to being the person your student needs.

In a sense, learning means stepping out into the unknown. Rachel Botsman, the author of *Who Can You Trust?*, describes trust as a 'confident relationship with the unknown'.[5] Many of our students have learned to be terrified of the unknown. In order, then, for our students to brave the unknown, they need a guide. This is where the tutor steps in. By coming alongside your student, by walking them through the

. . . .

4   See https://communityresearchcollaborative.org/relational-trust.
5   See https://twitter.com/rachelbotsman/status/960094497274081280?lang=en.

learning at a pace they can handle, you make learning possible and build their courage for independent learning in the future.

Imagine yourself as a Sherpa leading your student on a trek across a glacier. To you, the route is known and understood, whereas for the student it seems impassable. There are always rough moments with learning. They might find themselves on unsteady ground. They might panic and want to retreat. But you are there to help them push through, to find the most manageable and most direct route to the other side. Over time, they will learn to trust you and will be willing to take more and greater leaps into the unknown. When you think of yourself leading your student through challenging terrain, it becomes obvious how important it is that they trust you.

 Pause Point

How would you evaluate the relational trust in your tutoring relationships currently?

....

....

What are the principal reasons for this degree of trust, whether it is high or low? Try to be honest with yourself.

....

....

How can you take trust to the next level in your tutoring?

....

....

Chapter 7

WORKSHOP 4:
THE LEARNING LOOP

The initial conversations I have about a new student tend to go something like this. A parent will call and share that their child is struggling with maths. Their teacher is considering moving them down to the lowest set. They will ask whether I can help.

I will politely explore the terrain, asking what the teacher has said, how the student is doing in other subjects, what their school life has been like until now, their early childhood development and anything else that comes up in the conversation that seems relevant.

Then I will ask what they are hoping to achieve, which is always a tricky one. We can't make promises, but we do need to know what success would look like for this client. They might say that they want their child to keep up with the class or to fulfil their potential. Of course, if I were tutoring older students, I might have more specific goals, such as an exam pass or a top grade but, with the exception of test prep tutors, primary school tutors don't usually have the luxury of such clearly defined goals.

We usually agree that the goal is a happier and more confident learner. Building up the whole child is my favourite, if rather nebulous, objective. If you asked me what this looks like in practice, I might say the willingness to have a go at answering a question, a sense of curiosity or, even better, playfulness. The ultimate goal is to enable our students to become independent learners.

It can help to think of a tutor as a route planner. The first thing you enter is the destination and then your current location. With individualised planning, you can factor in barriers, shortcuts and pick-ups along the way. Sometimes you will choose the quickest route and sometimes you will choose a more circuitous route – stopping to smell the flowers and enjoy the journey. The route can be easily adjusted, but the start and end points tend to be locked in.

Deciding to take on a student shouldn't be a decision that you take lightly. If you have your doubts, that is okay. One of the most trustworthy things a tutor can do is to pass a student over to a colleague who is better matched to their needs. But, having understood and accepted the destination, you now become responsible for helping the student to get there. But how?

Back in Chapter 1, I introduced you to my three keys of effective tutoring. Having turned the first key, relationship, in Workshop 3, we are now going to learn how to use the second, responsiveness.

Responsiveness

I have asked the thousands of tutors with whom I am connected, 'What is the secret to effective planning?' Without exception, they all say 'responsiveness'. The consensus is overwhelming, and yet at the same time strangely unhelpful. Responsive to what, exactly?

In most mainstream schools, teachers spend the year sprinting to keep up with where they are supposed to be on the scheme of work. It is important to recognise this aspect of the school system because it helps us to understand our role as tutors and what ails many of our students today. They feel stressed and struggle to keep up. This is the backdrop for the consensus that tutoring must be responsive. It is a great relief for tutors and students to have the freedom to slow down, speed up or adjust the schedule without fear of judgement.

Responsiveness, then, is about seeing what the student needs and adapting the learning to provide it in the moment. If you are watching a student wrestle with a maths problem, you can support them then and there. Conversely, the minute I find my student confident with the work I have set, I will tell them to skip to the last section of the page so we can move on. In a classroom, I might have left them to complete the whole page and justified it by calling it practice, but in a tutoring session there are better things we can do with our time together.

In service to the newbies amongst us, I need to clarify still further. It takes time to develop a sense of what to respond to as well as how to respond. The guidance I have provided thus far won't help you if you don't know what you are looking for. Experienced tutors have an intuition which I will try to break down to help you get a feel for it.

The idea is to keep your students in a comfortable stretch – that is, within their zone of proximal development (ZPD). This term from educational psychologist Lev Vygotsky is a staple of teacher training courses.[1] It simply means to keep them reaching towards the next step in their learning, which they can manage with support or scaffolding. Once they have made it, you extend the stretch incrementally, as their ZPD rolls forward.

To return to the analogy of the gym: my personal trainer, Libby, from Chapter 2, was able to gauge my ability and then support me to extend myself safely. If she had pushed me too hard, I might have injured myself, lost trust in her or faith in myself. Equally, if the workout were too easy, I would have felt disappointed for underachieving. Libby had to find my ZPD, and she had to keep me there.

Some days I was tired, and other days I was on top form. Libby would adjust accordingly. Some exercises felt intimidating and others I loved. Libby knew how to mix them up. Sometimes my left knee ached, and she would effortlessly change the exercise, support my legs or work my core. Libby was in control, helping me to get to where I wanted to be – and I loved her for it. I felt safe and challenged at the same time.

. . . .

1   L. S. Vygotsky, *Mind in Society: The Development of Higher Psychological Processes* (Cambridge, MA: Harvard University Press, 1978).

Libby stood next to me, watching my responses, pushing me out of my comfort zone and into my ZPD. That is what a great tutor means when they say 'responsiveness'. They mean they are observing the student in the moment, interpreting their responses and adjusting for a perfect fit.

In this chapter, we will look at the core skills of teaching and learning within a framework I created called 'The Learning Loop' which has been inspired by the work of educationalist Ross Morrison McGill and his book *Mark, Plan, Teach*.[2] This is a responsive method of teaching that lends itself to long-term and short-term goals. It encompasses everything you will do in a tutoring session.

The four stages of the learning loop are assess, plan, teach and reassess. This is a sequence that you will repeat over and over again as you tutor, often without even noticing it. If this is all new to you, then there is a great deal of information here and you may have to go through these sections more than once. If you are a seasoned pro, I hope that by drawing your attention to what you do intuitively and unpicking why it works, we can take the mystery out of tutoring and help you to reach mastery.

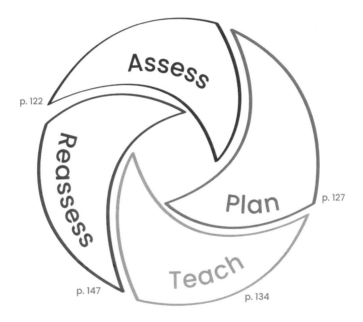

2   R. Morrison McGill, *Mark. Plan. Teach.* (London: Bloomsbury Education, 2017).

In this chapter, we will develop a broad understanding of the working parts of a tutoring session in a way that is practical and easy to apply. We will explore what to teach, how to teach it and how to know whether you have been successful. There are plenty of examples, so you can see how the ideas might apply to your specific context. We will tie in core pedagogical terms – such as mastery, feedback, pitch and pace, cognitive load and learning moments – and we will find out what the research tells us about what works well.

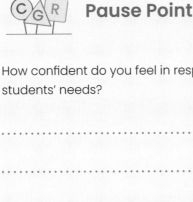 **Pause Point**

How confident do you feel in responding to your students' needs?

....

....

What are the challenges to being responsive, do you think?

....

....

What are the benefits of being responsive?

....

....

1. Assess

Since we are committed to being responsive, when we talk about assessment in tutoring, we are referring to a continuous process. You need accurate and up-to-date information about your student if you want to tailor your approach to their changing needs. Simply put, we assess to inform our planning. Constantly.

We are also thinking about the whole learner: how engaged they are in their learning and how they benefit as people, as well as their academic outcomes. We are using assessment to reflect on our own tutoring practice, using key performance indicators and accountability measures. It all sounds terribly serious, but in fact it is very intuitive. It is a mindset, and we will work through it together.

When it comes to assessment for learning, we are looking at three specific factors: knowledge, skills and beliefs. You need to explore what your student knows, what they can do and how they feel about it. You might have a student who has plenty of knowledge about a historical period but lacks essay-writing skills. Or a student who is capable in literary interpretation but struggles to memorise quotes from the text. Equally, you may have a student who hates studying French because someone once laughed at their accent. It is important to separate out these three elements as part of your assessment because it will help you to target your support more accurately.

I am assuming that you have the knowledge and skills required for your subject. If you need to brush up on these, especially in the context of examination boards, this should be part of your ongoing professional development. But you might be surprised to learn that inspiring confidence, or igniting motivation, is as much a part of the tutoring role as explaining long division. There is a wealth of knowledge out there about academic mentoring and coaching for well-being that you can explore if you feel this is an area that you need to develop.[3]

---

3   I have seen some excellent courses accredited by the International Coaching Federation: https://coachingfederation.org.

You need to explore what your student **knows**, what they **can do** and **how they feel about it**.

When it comes to assessment in tutoring, it usually makes sense to keep it light. There is no need to get too formal because it is just you and the student. There is one exception though: when preparing a student for exams it can help to recreate exam conditions to acclimatise them to timed, silent work.

Many tutors do an initial diagnostic test with their students. They find it useful to have a solid benchmark from which to measure progress and when reporting back to parents. For any sort of test or exam preparation, the best pre-test will be a past paper. This will give you a real-life basis from which to evaluate progress.

However, this type of approach doesn't tend to work with my own students, most of whom would be scared off by anything quite so formal. I, and many of the most confident tutors I know, take a more open-ended approach.

The first thing I do is chat: I get to know the young person and let them discover a little about me. Essentially, I am building the positive relationship that we discussed in Chapter 6. During this time, I find out how they feel about their studies and about their particular interests. Then, based on what I already know, I select some appropriate activities for them to tackle. If they find the material very hard or very easy, I will take it away or adapt it until I find the biting point. Remember the zone of proximal development. That is what you are looking for.

If you find the student is struggling, it is fine to help them along. This is a low-threat environment. You aren't trying to catch them out, and you certainly don't want to knock their confidence. In fact, once you have discovered where they are coming unstuck, you can jump right in and start supporting them.

Throughout this first assessment, you will be getting a feel for your student's confidence and their willingness to have a go. This will tell you a great deal about how they feel about the subject, and if their attitude could present a future barrier to learning. For example, maths anxiety is a recognised phenomenon. Learners can develop a negative emotional reaction to maths, which causes them to feel overwhelmed and stressed when faced with number problems. This can present a real long-term difficulty since functional maths skills are a prerequisite for most job applications. If you can avoid or alleviate maths anxiety by providing a comfortable and supportive environment in which your student can achieve and make progress, you will have made a lasting difference in their life.

In addition to the academic work and the coaching, there is another kind of continuous assessment that you will rely on heavily as a tutor. This is your assessment of your student's state of mind. As you get to know your student, you will learn to read their cues. You will learn to empathise and tune in when they are struggling and when they are bored. Ostensibly, you will learn to read their mind. This unspoken skill is an indicator of a successful tutor. The good news is that most children are easier to read than most adults. They have usually had less practice in hiding their feelings. However, you may have a student who is naturally shy or who has learned to be wary of adults. In this case, a lot of trust-building will need to happen.

Empathy is a core skill here. Try to put yourself in your student's shoes. What pressures or opportunities are they feeling? Are they engaged in the lesson? Are they ahead of you? Did you lose them a while back, and now they are worrying about how to ask you to go over it all again? How do they feel about the subject? How do they feel about you? We use this type of assessment all the time in social situations. You know what a bored person or an anxious person looks like. The difference is that, in a tutoring context, the bored or anxious person is your responsibility. It is up to you to wake them up or calm them down.

Try to expect more from a student than their prior attainment predicts. You might worry that you will be piling on too much pressure or aiming too high, but there are many robust studies which show that students achieve more when we expect more of them. This is called the Pygmalion effect, and there is a lovely anecdote in Sir John Jones' book, *The Magic-Weaving Business*, to illustrate it.

The story goes that a teacher was allocated the fourth set for GCSE maths. When the results arrived, she was asked to explain how she had got the fourth set to outperform the second set. The teacher replied, 'I thought I was teaching Set 2.' That is good, but the best part comes next. When asked if she would have changed anything, she said that she wished she'd thought they were the top set.[4]

Pause Point

What assessments do you currently use with your students, formally and informally?

· ·

· ·

How helpful are each of these methods? How could you improve your use of assessment?

· ·

· ·

What are your expectations of your students? How might these be affecting their outcomes?

· ·

· ·

4 J. Jones, *The Magic-Weaving Business: Finding the Heart of Learning and Teaching* (Stradbally, Co. Waterford: Leannta Publishing, 2011), p. 89.

2. Plan

Fail to plan; plan to fail. You need to have a full session planned, even if you end up scrapping it at the last minute to help your student complete an urgent piece of homework. There is a world of difference between being flexible and winging it. Think about your learning goals and the route you have planned, and keep moving forward at whatever pace your student needs.

Learning Objectives

In the last couple of decades, it has become common practice for teachers to write learning objectives on the board at the beginning of every lesson. I have seen teachers fail inspections for forgetting to do so. This is probably excessive, but writing the learning objective on the board is not just another administrative task for an already overburdened teacher. In fact, it is a powerful teaching strategy.

Imagine that I wrote on the board: 'By the end of this lesson, my student will be able to recite their seven times table backwards.' Assuming it is the right goal, this simple statement gives shape to the entire session. I can imagine the multiplication games and activities we will play. I can imagine testing the student repeatedly. I can imagine the sense of accomplishment when they finally manage it. And so can they.

By setting a well-defined learning objective, everyone knows where they are going. You can draw a straight line from your starting point to your end point and ignore all the distractions. Your student needs to know what the objectives are so that they can actively participate in achieving them.

As we know, education is not done to a child; it is done with them. If you and your student are clear about the goals, you are more likely to reach them – together.

Learning Activities

There are only three types of learning activity. Anything you could do in a session will boil down to acquiring, revising or applying knowledge, skills or beliefs. Understanding these three types of activity should help you to select your planning with more clarity.[5]

Acquire

Acquire activities involve the assimilation of new information. This is when the student learns something they didn't know before. Note that I didn't say 'for the first time'. This is because they might have viewed the material many times before but it didn't stick. To avoid this happening yet again, here are some principles to ensure your student successfully acquires the learning.

1   **Be sure that it is a teaching moment.** A teaching moment is when the stars align and your student is mentally, physically and emotionally available to learn from you. Teaching moments don't feel rushed, heavy or pressurised. They feel light and calm. They don't come right at the beginning or end of a tutoring session, when your student is coming down with a cold, when good weather or a snow day is beckoning, or when it is noisy next door, or when they are hungry, upset or agitated.

Use that core skill of empathy to assess whether it is a learning moment. If it isn't, don't push through with a new piece of knowledge; take your session outdoors, sort out the noisy neighbours or grab a packet of biscuits. If your student isn't receptive, the information won't stick and the learning will have negative connotations the next time you try to cover it. Instead, switch to a revise or apply activity (more on these below) and circle back for another go a bit later. That is the freedom of tutoring! Being able to recognise and create teaching moments is a vital skill. Lean into the 7Ps of Professionalism to achieve these moments.

---

5   This idea is based on the work of Benjamin Bloom and his Taxonomy of Learning.

Warning: it is very difficult to step away from your plan if you discover it isn't a teaching moment. It may feel like failure but, in fact, it is a sign of being extremely attentive, flexible and trustworthy.

2   **Be super-clear.** If you muddle a student you could really knock their confidence. You will make them feel that the topic is too hard for them to understand and create resistance to learning, which is much harder to undo than to avoid. Clarity is crucial, so try to rehearse the new topic before you deliver it. This is about more than planning; it is about practising. If you explain the information out loud a few times before your session, you will find that it will become clearer and more fluent. The time spent thinking through a new topic is time extremely well spent. If you are tutoring outside of your subject specialism, and many of us do from time to time, you will need to do a lot of reading around to deliver the topic with assurance. Communicating confidence is crucial to your student accepting the information. Although you don't need to be infallible, they need to trust that you know your subject well and that you are going to make it accessible to them.

3   **Give context.** Students need schemas in their long-term memory if they are to going to assimilate new knowledge in a way that makes powerful connections. In other words, people who know stuff find it easier to learn more stuff; unfortunately, the opposite is also true. Mary Myatt talks about the importance of building a student's 'intellectual architecture'.[6] When we demonstrate how new ideas relate to existing ones, we help our students to organise the storeroom of their mind. This helps them to recall and apply their learning in the future. Before you introduce new information, remind them about related learning that is already secure, then show them how the new idea fits in relation to what they already know and can do.

---

6   M. Myatt, Intellectual Architecture [blog] (22 June 2023). Available at: https://www.marymyatt.com/blog/intellectual-architecture.

Revise

Retrieval practice is a technique for embedding knowledge in our long-term memories and ensuring that we can find it when we need it. According to psychologist Jeffrey Karpicke: 'Every time a memory is retrieved, that memory becomes more accessible in the future.'[7] If you want your student to remember what they have learned, you must include the opportunity for them to retrieve prior knowledge and skills.

It usually makes sense to set a revise activity at the beginning of the session, as it helps the student to warm up and gets them ready for an acquire activity.

Revise activities are endlessly adaptable; they can be as imaginative as you like. Examples of retrieval exercises include quizzes and tests, cloze texts (also known as gap-fills), singing/chanting and brain dumps (any kind of note-taking where you write down as much as you know on a subject). It could be a card game that involves matching key words to definitions, a mind map explaining the drivers of the American Revolution or a favourite song that goes over number bonds to ten. The important point is that it includes nothing new. Revise activities should feel like limbering up or a comfortable stretch.

There is a saying: 'Don't practice until you get it right. Practice until you can't get it wrong'. In the UK, the mastery approach is better established in sports and music than in academic study. We can imagine it in the way that a pianist will go over the same four bars for hours or a swimmer will practise their flip turns endlessly. Mastery is achieved by repeating each grain of learning until it is as deeply embedded in your memory as your best friend's phone number. Purposeful practice, brought into mainstream consciousness by author Malcolm Gladwell and developed further by journalist and Olympic table tennis player Matthew Syed, is the idea that repetition

---

7   J. D. Karpicke, A Powerful Way to Improve Learning and Memory. *Psychological Science Agenda*, 30(6) (2016).

results in mastery.[8] Or, as my 9-year-old daughter's teacher says, 'Practice makes progress'.

Like a sportsperson or musician, isolate one move and work on it tirelessly until your student cracks it. If they need to crack introductions to history essays, don't make them write essay after essay – just concentrate on introductions. Analyse good and bad examples until they understand what makes an effective introduction, and then practice, practice, practice, writing only introductions until they flow effortlessly.

Most students aren't used to working in this way, so you will need to make the learning feel fun, purposeful and comfortable if you want to work them this hard. However, a motivated student – if they can get a feel for this kind of work – will have a real chance not just to reach a goal but to master their subject.

Apply

Apply activities are predicated on knowledge and understanding. Revising can happen out of context, whilst applying is about putting learning back into context, which is important for the larger goal of building intellectual architecture.

Give your student plenty of opportunities to apply their knowledge in order to increase fluency. You can also enrich learning by encouraging them to apply their knowledge and skills in real-life contexts. For example, they could write a formal letter to the council about the state of the local park and post it. They could double a recipe and measure out the ingredients for a cake or smoothie. They could complete a GCSE past paper. It can also be powerful to use genuine texts rather than teaching resources, which takes learning out of the theoretical and into the practical. The point is not so your student can understand the real world in the future; it is so they can engage with it right now.

Enable your students to show you what they have learned by inviting them to apply their knowledge to new and complex problems. I think

8   See M. Gladwell, *Outliers: The Story of Success* (New York: Little, Brown & Co., 2008); and M. Syed, *Bounce: The Myth of Talent and the Power of Practice* (London: Fourth Estate, 2011).

of it as planting a bulb in the soil in autumn and seeing it bloom in the spring, independent and beautiful.

Don't forget to consider your students' concentration spans. Try to mix up activities every twenty to thirty minutes to make the most of your time. If you are focusing on one history essay throughout the session, think about working with the material in a variety of ways – for example, writing, analysing, editing and comparing. When tutoring primary-age children, it can make sense to do a combination of reading, writing and maths in each session. You don't need to give all three equal weighting; that decision should be based on your learning goals.

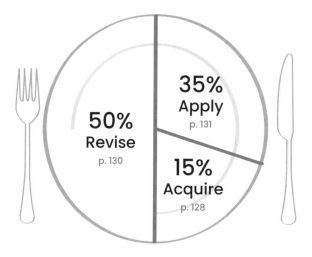

I like to use this figure of a 'healthy diet' in tutor training, simply to draw tutors' attention to how much of each activity they plan to use. However, just as in food science, there are many opinions about the correct balance of the different groups, and there are many right ways based on the unique needs of your learner in that session. For instance, you may have covered all the new material and mostly be on to revising, or you may give over a whole session to application, such as an extended writing activity. You get to decide what you serve your students. Choose wisely.

Group Tuition

The financial benefits of offering group tuition are compelling. It's an efficient way of increasing your income whilst maintaining the same working hours. The pedagogical benefits are immense too.

In addition to being more affordable for parents, small group tuition at its best combines the personalisation of one-to-one tuition with the power of group feedback, peer assessment and collaborative learning.

If you are considering delivering your sessions to groups as well as, or instead of, one-to-ones, you're in great company. Many very successful tutors choose this route. It works particularly well for exam preparation. It may be less good for supporting students with specific needs, although in some cases the peer interaction can be a valuable learning opportunity.

To do group tuition well, you need to approach it differently to either one-to-one tutoring or classroom teaching. You need to consider how to set up the group so that the students benefit from working with each other as well as working with you. Rather than mimicking the classroom situation where, for much of the time, thirty children are vying for the attention of one teacher, create a context where the students interact with each other as much as possible.

Consider all the relationships in the group as potential assets. Give plenty of opportunities for collaboration and peer assessment. Let the power of the collective become something that is really felt.

Of course, planning for groups requires you to structure activities which challenge and support each individual in a way that gets them motivated and making progress. Yes, this is a tall order, and one which needs plenty of consideration and development. But when done well, the results can be remarkable.

Pause Point

Have a look online and choose a session planner template that includes learning objectives, learning outcomes, timings, resources, teaching points, considerations for inclusion and opportunities for assessment. If you don't find one that seems right, create your own.

Create a session incorporating the three different activity types. Consider how much time you will give to each one, and in which order you will deliver them.

How do these plans compare with what you have been doing until now?

....

....

3. Teach

Teaching books and journals explore many great techniques for teaching and learning. I am only focusing on those ideas that are most applicable for tutoring. Whilst most strategies will work at any level and in any subject, some will be better suited to you and your student. With any or all of these approaches, it is worth doing your own research or talking with other tutors about how they use them in practice.

Facilitating vs. Instructing

When you think about your tutoring, are you more of a guide on the side or a sage on the stage – that is, do you facilitate or do you lecture? Most of the time, a tutor is in the enviable position of guiding from the sidelines – holding space and supporting the student like a coach, an early years practitioner or even a Montessori teacher. Literally and figuratively, you sit alongside your student, watching their progress and helping them as needed.

However, there are times, usually during an acquire activity, when your student will need you to explain the topic to them. This is when you will switch into instructional mode, become the sage and, keeping in mind all the techniques we have learned in the planning section, clearly and effectively steer them through the material.

The tutor's role is usually more facilitative than authoritative. We tend to talk with, rather than talk at, our students. The crowd management that dominates the classroom learning experience is redundant, and teaching becomes that wonderfully close-up view of what the student needs to learn *now*. And *now*. And *now*.

Facilitating is a specific discipline. It requires self-restraint. By the time you get to the teaching stage, you have done most of the hard work. Now, you can take a back seat and allow the student to take the lead. Your role is to prompt, challenge or support. As an enabler, you will help your student to stay on task and to get as much from the activity as possible.

Pitch and Pace

We've discussed the power of precision in tutoring, and, conversely, the lack of precision in some classroom contexts. Tutors do what most teachers wish they could: tutors can adapt the pitch, i.e. how simple or complex the work is, and the pace, i.e. how fast or slow you go, to the needs of each student.

There are some students who process information particularly slowly. That is, they have no problem with the material, but the speed at which most classes move is too quick for them. They are constantly left behind and that reflects in their outcomes and their self-esteem. There are also students who are very quick on the uptake, and they tend to become disruptive or disengaged whilst they wait for the rest of the class to catch on. With a tutor, neither of these types of students should have an issue, since you will be able to see how confident they are with the material and adapt the work accordingly.

Equally, the best fit approach of most classrooms, where teachers 'pitch' the level of work to the middle attaining group, or slightly higher, and then differentiate up and down with adapted work is nothing compared to the comfortable, open-ended fit you can find with each of your students as a tutor. Since our planning is always informed by our assessment, and we are committed to changing this as frequently as necessary.

Even the most competent student will be weak in certain areas, and the least successful students will have places where they excel. As their tutor, you can notice these strengths and weaknesses and adapt to address each one specifically. This will not only mean that the student makes better progress since the work is ideally tailored to their needs, but it also means that the student will find the learning far more comfortable, since it will stretch and support them in all the right places.

Concrete, Pictorial, Abstract

The concrete, pictorial, abstract (CPA) approach was developed by American psychologist Jerome Bruner in the 1960s to help children learn about abstract mathematical concepts, but it can be used as a scaffold in any subject. It might mean that at the start of a unit on shape, space and measure, for example, you would do a lot of pouring and measuring with real-life objects. The aim is for your student to get a material sense of the meaning behind the maths. Once they have grasped the concrete, you can move on to the pictorial. These might be labelled drawings of buckets from which your student can simply read the scale to find the answer. Finally, you will move to the abstract, which in this case would be calculations that find the answer without using any visual prompts.

The single biggest rule with CPA, which you can build into a philosophy if you like, is to stay with the concrete for as long as possible. Maths gets mysterious and scary for students when it moves to the abstract; the pictorial stage is a wonderful scaffold between the two. All the best maths tutors rely on concrete maths resources because they know that exploring algebra tiles, Dienes blocks, Cuisenaire rods, geoboards and simple counters is the best way to build a student's mathematical understanding. If you are tutoring maths online, there are some fantastic programmes (such as MathsBot.com) that simulate each of these resources.

However, for all my passion and excitement about concrete maths manipulatives, very few of us who tutor were taught using these tools. If they were in your classroom growing up, their use would probably have been limited to the 'low ability' tables, which was unlikely to be you if you are teaching maths today. Ironically, those of us in the higher streamed groups lost out by not having a chance to build concrete mathematical concepts. If you are intrigued and think this may be helpful to your students, do some research about the CPA approach and find some training on maths manipulatives. Then have a go and let yourself play.

Dual Coding

Dual coding is combining pictures with text to help learners understand and remember. This could mean linking your spoken or written text with drawings or diagrams. You could use mind maps, sketchnotes or, as I like to do, you can create visual models of the concepts.

A word of warning though. The goal is to simplify the concepts and make them memorable, so be careful that your visuals don't overwhelm your student by accident. Don't use too many words on a slide and make sure you give students enough time to have a good look at any visuals you put in front of them.

What is the best way to find out if your use of dual coding is a help or a hindrance? Ask your student, of course! Then, give them the time and space to create pictorial representations of the work you do together. It is not a frivolous use of your tutoring time. It is a legitimate approach, and can be a lot of fun.

Tell a Story

Our minds love stories. You can use stories to help your student stay engaged and bring your subject to life. This is pretty straight-forward if you are teaching history, but if it is science or philosophy you will need to be more creative. True stories tend to be the most powerful, so it may be worth sharing some background on the scientists alongside their scientific discoveries. And if you are teaching Mandarin, simply telling a terrific story in Mandarin should motivate your student to keep up.

Powerful Feedback

As world-renowned educational researcher Professor John Hattie has observed, the problem with learning is that it is invisible. Minds are not like a car engine: we can't lift the hood on our students' learning and see the motor whirring. Instead, we can only see its results of learning. Like gravity, learning is intangible, but its results are concrete. Unfortunately, it is not as predictable as gravity. I know that every time I throw a ball it will fall. I don't know that every time I read new information I will learn it.

That is why there is a growing body of research aiming to understand what works best in teaching and learning. Do children learn better in ability groupings or mixed groups? Does holding a child down a year affect their development? Does an arts education improve overall outcomes?

One of our **goals** as tutors is to teach our students to **become independent learners.**

When we want to plan how and where to invest our time and money in education, resources like the Education Endowment Foundation's Teaching and Learning Toolkit can be invaluable because it makes the research accessible and easy to understand.[9] Fortunately for us, most of the best recommendations for interventions lend themselves brilliantly to tutoring – for example, one-to-one tuition ranks high at five months' impact. When taken together with the highest ranking interventions – feedback (eight months' impact), metacognition and self-regulation (seven months' impact) – you can see how great your opportunity is to make a real difference to your students.

Professor John Hattie has observed that 'The simplest prescription for improving education must be "dollops of feedback".'[10] The evidence shows that feedback is the single most effective intervention in teaching.[11] Tutors are at an enormous advantage because our feedback can be as immediate and supportive as we choose. As it is such a powerful tool, we should think carefully about how we use it to best effect, depending on the student and where they are in the learning process.

I think of effective feedback using two metaphors. The first is the reflective studs or cat's eyes used to signal the lanes on a road. They light up your way in the dark, keep you on track and move you towards your destination. Not only do these clever little devices show you where you are supposed to be, but when you veer out of lane and accidentally drive over them, you will feel and hear the bump-bump-bump of the metal studs. They will continue making that annoying sound until you make a correction and move back to the centre of the lane. The second is the bumpers in a bowling lane which stop your ball from dropping into the gutter, no matter how bad your aim. They prevent failure in a way that the reflective studs don't.

- -

9   See https://educationendowmentfoundation.org.uk/education-evidence/
     teaching-learning-toolkit.
10 J. Hattie, Measuring the Effects of Schooling. *Australian Journal of Education*,
     36(1) (1992), 5–13. Available at: https://www.nzcer.org.nz/nzcerpress/set/articles/
     measuring-effects-schooling.
11 See https://educationendowmentfoundation.org.uk/education-evidence/
     teaching-learning-toolkit/feedback.

Think about your use of feedback in supporting different students at different points. When should you be cat's eyes – pointing the way, alerting them to their mistakes but not intervening? And when should you be bumpers – not allowing them to fall and never letting failure be an option?

Of course, there is a time and a place for not allowing your students to fail and for helping them every step of the way, but you don't want to stay there too long. One of our goals as tutors is to teach our students to become independent learners. Risk-taking is part of the process. If you can't fail, how meaningful is your success?

What does effective feedback look like in practice? When should we hover over every sentence, and when should we hold our peace and see if they go back to correct themselves?

In my view, you want to be bumpers when it comes to introducing new knowledge and cat's eyes when you are working on embedding or applying information. In other words, be generous with your corrective feedback when you are introducing new material – you don't want your students to form misconceptions about new knowledge – but take a moment before you give corrective feedback during a revise or apply activity.

Also remember to give plenty of specific positive feedback. It is immensely motivating and at least as instructive as corrective feedback when done well. Positive feedback is not praise for the person ('You're so clever!'); it is praise targeted on a learning behaviour ('Well done for persevering with that tricky problem').

There is a lovely video called 'Austin's Butterfly', which tells the story of the class of a first-grade student, Austin, who is working on copying a photograph of a butterfly. Over six iterations, Austin works and reworks his drawing, based on the critique of his classmates, until finally he produces a very accurate copy of the original. Of course, not every drawing is better than the last; progress happens in fits and starts. Throughout the video, Ron Berger shows that within a culture of peer support and feedback, Austin can produce something way beyond most expectations.[12]

12   See https://modelsofexcellence.eleducation.org/resources/austins-butterfly.

I first watched this video at a teacher training event run by the wonderful Mary Myatt, author of *High Challenge, Low Threat*. In a room of a hundred teachers or more, most agreed that they would have accepted Austin's first draft of the butterfly. They wouldn't have pushed him through so many edits to create something of which he could be really proud. Instead, they would have told him to move on to drawing the next minibeast.

What is the message for us as tutors? Remember the Pygmalion effect: raise your expectations way above what is usual for your student and then give them the feedback to help them get there.

For tutor training, I created a model based on the acronym TEAMS, which stands for: timely, encouraging, accurate, measured and safe. This is a simple acronym to help you think about best practice when giving effective feedback to your students.

- **Timely.** When is the right time to give feedback? Is it immediately, at the end of a piece of work or something in-between? As with most things in tutoring, the answer is 'it depends'. Sometimes you want to correct your student immediately if they have forgotten a full stop, and sometimes you may want to wait until they finish the paragraph to see whether they go back, reread and add the full stops themselves.

  Getting the timing right requires considerable judgement on your part. You need to know when and whether your student is ready for feedback, based on your ongoing assessment of their state of mind and your clear understanding of their learning goals.

- **Encouraging.** The common fail in feedback is too much negativity. Your feedback must always help your student to move forward; it must never knock them down. Make sure you pay attention and critique what the student has done well as well as what they need to improve on for next time. Find ways to show them that you believe in them, and that you know they can keep on improving.

- **Accurate.** Your feedback must be accurately informed by assessment and based on what they can do next.

- **Measured.** Don't overwhelm your students with your feedback. Give them just as much as they can cope with and save the rest for the next session.

- **Safe.** It is important to give feedback in a safe space. If you are working in an online group, you may want to speak to the student privately using the chat function. If you want to give feedback for the benefit of the group, then consider anonymising it, and always get the student's consent. There are lots of ways to ensure that you save a student's face when you give feedback, whether it is positive or negative. Feedback should not create competition between your students. It must feel good and provide a safe growing space for them to learn together. It goes without saying that your students shouldn't feel criticised or shamed in any way, but it can happen so easily. There is so much skill in giving feedback that you can develop along the way.

A final note on feedback and its central role in the learning process. You student is always responding to feedback, whether explicit or implied. This is true in the work they produce and in their beliefs. They are constantly reading you and responding to your signals, which is why the 7Ps of Professionalism are so important. So much of your power and influence lies in your feedback – the smile, the frown and the adjustments you make.

Self-Regulated Learning

Alongside feedback, metacognition and self-regulation are two of the best evidenced interventions for improving learning.[13] We have discovered that when we give students the tools to reflect on their learning, we transform their power as learners.

---

13   See https://educationendowmentfoundation.org.uk/education-evidence/ teaching-learning-toolkit/metacognition-and-self-regulation.

Metacognition and self-regulation – or 'thinking about thinking' and 'learning about learning' – are amongst the most powerful tools we can give to our students. To be able to reflect on where we are up to in our learning and how we can help ourselves move forward is the greatest learning power of them all. Everything beyond that, as they say, is commentary.

Metacognition and self-regulation sound very complicated, but they are something we do all the time – for example, when we write a shopping list so we don't forget things. These are moments when we notice ourselves thinking – or forgetting – and we discover strategies for supporting our own minds. How many of us have learned to retrace our steps until we remember what we were looking for? How many of us, when we can't find some paper, will go to the shops knowing there are five things on our list, three at the supermarket and two at the pharmacy? We help ourselves to organise our thinking all day long, and it is extremely helpful.

My 6-year-old daughter was practising some spelling words recently. She went through them all with such enthusiasm that at the end I said, 'Wow! You know those words so well!' She replied, 'Yes, except this one, this one and that one.' Then she looked at those three again. It is true – she is a remarkable person. But the ability to look honestly at what we can and can't do is natural and integral to our development. A toddler knows when they have cracked walking. A child knows when they have mastered riding a bike. Unfortunately, most of us lose this talent for learning as we get older. We put up shields to protect ourselves from failure and disappointment. We forget that falling down is part of the process of growing up.

One of the best gifts we can give our students is the understanding that, yes, it will be tough, but, yes you can manage it – just as you have so many times before.

We can help our students to benefit by:

- **Planning for learning.** Teach your student to plan ahead – for example, with a revision timetable.

- **Mnemonics and procedures.** By teaching 'Big elephants can always understand small elephants' (the spelling mnemonic for 'because') or 'I ate and I ate and was sick on the floor' (8 x 8 = 64), you can train your students to create mental hooks for their learning. You can encourage them to say their spellings aloud, pronouncing all the unexpected letters (as in the first 'r' in February) or to make up their own mnemonics for anything they will need to memorise for exams.

- **Resilience and autonomy.** It is helpful to point out to your students what is really going on – for example, by saying, 'You tend to struggle with this bit' or 'You seem a bit worried about that topic,' you give them the language and opportunity to interrogate their own thinking. They can then reflect on what is worrying them and address it. 'I missed lunch, so I might find it hard to concentrate if we don't get hold of some biscuits' is a brilliant example of a student knowing how they learn and taking responsibility for their own needs.

Model and Scaffold Towards Success

The longest-running children's TV programme in the world is *Blue Peter*. Amongst other segments on the show, the fresh-faced presenters teach viewers how to make various cookery and craft projects using common household objects. Before starting the step-by-step process, they bring out a completed version of the model saying, 'Here's one I made earlier.'

This is modelling and scaffolding at its best. The final product is the model, showing children what, ideally, they will have created by the end of the process. The stepped guidance is the scaffold, providing structure to ensure the children have a good chance of making something resembling the model.

Anything you want your student to complete successfully requires a model and a scaffold. Depending on their individual needs, the scaffold can be structured (like a step-by-step guide or a planning frame) or loose (such as reminders, questioning and feedback). The trick with scaffolds, as in construction, is that they are only there to guide and enable. If they are more supportive than the student needs, they can reduce independence.

The aim of a scaffold is to help the student reach the next level, guide their steps and reduce the need to leap. A great example of a scaffold is the training wheels on a bicycle. The child may have started out riding a tricycle, with three wheels firmly on the ground, so when they first switch up to a bike, they expect the training wheels to give them the same sense of stability. In fact, they do not and must not. The stabilisers offer some reassurance, but they should also force the child to sit up, pedal harder and find their balance. Ultimately, stabilisers should make themselves redundant.

Consider using scaffolds that a student can take away with them in their mind. What sets of questions, reminders or learning techniques could you give your student to guide their work, even when you aren't there?

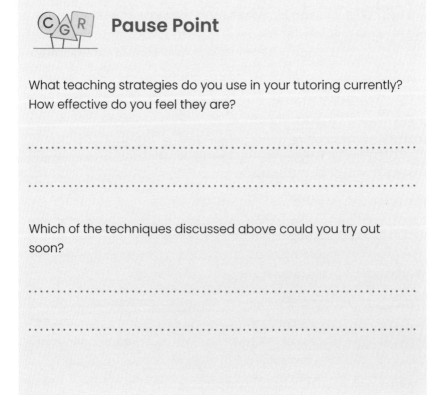

Pause Point

What teaching strategies do you use in your tutoring currently? How effective do you feel they are?

....

....

Which of the techniques discussed above could you try out soon?

....

....

How would you know whether they have worked well?

....

....

4. Reassess

Reassessment is where we check in to see how our student is doing. As we have seen, this process is constant and almost imperceptible. We complete learning loops again and again throughout sessions and across sessions. We discover a misconception, re-explain the concept and then reassess the student's understanding in the moment. Every time we respond to our student by speeding up, slowing down, pausing for a break or clarifying an explanation, it is reassessment. Using this mindset of continuous assessment, the assess/reassess stages blur into one, so assessment is constantly informing planning and teaching in a fluid process.

To describe this approach, leadership theorists use the phrase 'be a thermostat, not a thermometer'. Whilst a thermometer merely reads the temperature, a thermostat uses that reading to adjust the temperature to optimise the environment. Tutors operate like a thermostat: by responding to an ongoing assessment of how our student is progressing (and feeling) we can make continual improvements. We might adjust our pitch or our pace. We might change the scheduling or the learning environment. Or we may need to change nothing at all. The point is that we are taking responsibility for the learning needs of our student.

Amanda Cremona, a SEND tutor, shared with me that one of her students seemed unusually sulky and disengaged during a session. Based on the success of the previous session, Amanda had moved the work up a level because she had done so well, but clearly the jump felt too big to the student and the activity too hard. The student's resistance told Amanda that her confidence had been knocked. She modified the activity immediately to redirect the learning and re-engage the student. It took a while, but by the end of the session, the energy was back up and the student felt reassured. It didn't take a term or a week or even an hour to make the change. Amanda didn't waste a single moment. She read the temperature and responded immediately.

In committing to being responsive, a tutor must keep their eye firmly on the student. Since we have the luxury to assess and adjust constantly, we can intervene instantaneously, which is what makes tutoring so efficient. Reassessment can be one of a tutor's superpowers. When we get really good at being responsive, the learning can seem effortless to the student because it is always a good fit.

Reflective Practice

We have come to the final key in our three keys of effective tutoring model: reflectiveness. Being a reflective practitioner is one of the core tenets for any professional educator – in fact, for any professional. Reflectiveness is what keeps us honest and growing. It is the skill of regularly asking ourselves: 'How did that go? What made it so successful? How could it have been better? What could I do differently next time?' In the case of tutoring, if we don't ask ourselves these questions, maybe no one will.

But reflective practice isn't easy. We tend to slip into negative self-talk very readily. We might say, 'I always make the same mistake' rather than the more constructive, 'There seems to be a pattern here.' Or, 'I'm just not cut out for this' rather than asking, 'Which part of this do I have the control to change?' It is therefore one of the three keys of being an effective tutor and possibly the most difficult.

To be a reflective practitioner, you need to feel safe, skilled and supported. You need to have a safe space to ask yourself difficult questions, you need to be confident enough to answer truthfully and you need to be supported by others who can help you to find the answers. In the Qualified Tutor community, we have group coaching to provide this support. Through a structured programme led by expert coaches, we organise high-trust group sessions where tutors of every specialism do their thinking and talk through their issues. They lean on the 'hive mind', or shared knowledge, to find solutions and obtain guidance. Tutors say that it leaves them feeling centred and gives them a chance to discuss ideas they would never otherwise have had the confidence to explore.

To do your best work, you need to develop a practice for reflectiveness. You could find a coach, you could journal or you could find an accountability partner. There are many ways to make it happen, but make sure you do. It will transform your practice and give you the assurance and clarity you need to keep going. By creating a reflective practice, you can be sure that you are doing your best for your students, and you can help yourself to continually improve.

Double-Loop Learning

It is said that the definition of insanity is doing the same thing over and over again and expecting different results. That is single-loop learning: you try, try and try again.

In double-loop learning, head teacher and author Viviane Robinson invites us to go right back to the planning stage.[14] Query the learning objective: was the student ready for this goal, or do you need to go back in order to go forward? Query the method: did the method not suit the student? What other method would? Query the delivery: consider the pitch, the pace and whether it was a teaching moment. Did you model and scaffold? Was your feedback specific enough? The responsive cycle of the learning loop is designed to enable you to be open-minded, reflective and resilient.

. . . .

14   V. Robinson, *Capabilities Required for Leading Improvement: Challenges for Researchers and Developers* [paper presentation]. Research Conference 2017: Leadership for Improving Learning – Insights from Research (Camberwell, VIC: Australian Council for Educational Research, 2017), pp. 1–5. Available at: https://research.acer.edu.au/research_conference/RC2017/28august/2.

As we've said, learning isn't linear. It is a process: progressive but unpredictable. It can plateau, accelerate or stall. I imagine progress like a line graph that might chart the growth of a business. Growth (and in our case learning) happens in fits and starts – but if the environment is supportive, there will be an overall upwards trajectory.

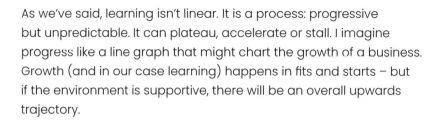

Pause Point

Go back to the Pause Point at the beginning of this workshop where I asked you how confident you are that your tutoring is effective, what better would look like and how would you know whether you had achieved this. Now, consider what teaching strategies you might try to use to boost the effectiveness of your tutoring. Make a plan for how you might implement this based on the following questions:

Who will you try this new approach with? What will you do? When will you do it?

....

....

Where might you anticipate problems? How can you mitigate for those problems?

....

....

How will you evaluate this experiment?

....

....

Chapter 8

WORKSHOP 5: BARRIERS TO LEARNING

Special Educational Needs, Mental Health and Well-Being

At 43 years old, it occurred to me that I might have attention deficit hyperactivity disorder (ADHD). I had been struggling to organise my time, manage my daily life and regulate my emotions. I had worked so hard that I had burned out. I was depleted and struggling with depression and anxiety. At my lowest, I lay in bed at two o'clock on a Tuesday afternoon. Texting my friend, Jack, I wrote: 'I think I broke my brain.' That is really what it felt like.

An assessment confirmed that I do fit the ADHD profile. That was when I learned to ask for help. Like wiping away steam from a bathroom mirror, I could suddenly see myself more clearly. My children have a mother who will read them endless stories, dance around the kitchen and cuddle them for hours, but never, not once, have we practised times tables or spellings. Raising five children I can do, but signing their homework books is sheer agony.

Exploring the ADHD literature was bemusing at first. Surely everyone struggles in these ways? Surely this was the universal human experience? Then I realised it was because I spend so much of my time with people who are like me. Those of us who love tutoring tend to be restless, sensitive, intuitive and enthusiastic. We don't love crowds but we do love people. We get stuck in our own heads and down rabbit holes. We are perfectly imperfect, and so are the students with whom we work.

There is a lot of excellent material out there about supporting learners with special educational needs. For me, it starts with educator Dame Alison Peacock's phrase 'learning without limits'.[1] Our biggest commitment as tutors is believing in our students – believing they can excel and exceed expectations. This isn't rhetoric. We know that our expectations have an immense impact on learner outcomes; we discussed the Pygmalion effect in Chapter 7. Equally, our lack of expectations can be their biggest barrier to learning. So, the first thing we need to commit to as tutors is the unshakeable belief that our students' abilities are limitless.

Learning without limits is a philosophy and a commitment to inclusive practice that can be deeply rewarding and inspiring. Melissa Harvey, our governess archetype from Chapter 2, now a 38-year-old linguist, mum and full-time tutor, told me about a 16-year-old student with whom she had started working a few weeks earlier.

He's sitting GCSEs. I only met him at Easter, but had I met his family years ago, I believe it would have been a much different path. He's struggling through these exams that are completely inaccessible to him, and it literally breaks my heart. But here we are with a few weeks to go. All I could do is try and help, and that's what we're doing. He had failed his functional skills maths a few months ago, but when we got the news last week that he'd passed his Level 3 functional maths, I nearly cried.

Honestly, I think that probably means more to me than if I get a call from one of my students with the 8s, the 9s and the A stars. For me, this young man has made my year because I have made a difference. It's all credit to him and his hard work. You don't sit the exams for them, but I know I've helped, and that's really special.

---

1   A. Peacock, Learning Without Limits, *TEDxNorwichED* [video] (28 March 2016). Available at: https://www.youtube.com/watch?v=8oxxPi6c-Nw.

What are the best learning goals for our students? The guiding question, especially with learners with exceptional needs, should always be: what do they really need to learn next? Achieving functional skills in maths and English may be the most beneficial focus for students who struggle academically because we need them in everyday life, alongside life skills such as communication, self-care and confidence building. Depending on your remit as a tutor, you may find that 'to be able to make a cup of tea safely' is the best objective for a session.

The focus here is on a commitment to the best development of the learner rather than specific learning outcomes. Learning without limits doesn't ask you to push a dyslexic student through entrance exams with no regard to their particular challenges, but it may mean ensuring they have the right access arrangements and reasonable adjustments to show what they know and can do.

Alongside our 'learning without limits' mindset, it is helpful to consider the difference between equality and equity. 'Equality means each individual or group of people is given the same resources or opportunities. Equity recognizes that each person has different circumstances and allocates the exact resources and opportunities needed to reach an equal outcome.'[2] This is where skill comes in. If we are to give all our students a fair chance, we must provide for each of them in the way that they need. To do this, we need to know them, their unique set of needs and what resources are available to support them.

The development of assistive technologies for students with additional needs is ever evolving. It is an exciting space to explore. However, it is not being adopted by mainstream education at the pace that many believe it could and should be. This is probably due to a lack of resourcing and, as always, a lack of headspace. I once worked with a Year 6 student who was unable to read the end-of-year exam paper. However, once we had set her up with a smart reader pen – a pen-shaped device that would scan the text

. . . .

2   Milken Institute School of Public Health, Equity vs. Equality: What's the Difference? *George Washington University* (5 November 2020). Available at: https://onlinepublichealth.gwu.edu/resources/equity-vs-equality/.

and read it aloud to her via discreet earphones – she was able to provide answers to the questions through a scribe.

This is where tutors come into their own. The wonderful SEND tutor Amanda Cremona from Workshop 4 who realised that she had overstretched a student and adjusted her pitch immediately, is constantly exploring what tech is out there to support her learners. She tests out resources with her students and then introduces them to schools. Endlessly frustrated with the sluggish adoption of assistive technology in some SEND departments, she is single-handedly making a change in the school communities with which she works.

Once you have identified the specific needs of your students, be proactive and seek out the right resources to support them. Inclusive practice means everything from noise-cancelling headphones to textbooks that represent diverse groups.

I recently worked with a maths tutor who said that inclusive practice wasn't relevant to him because he didn't teach special needs. I patiently explained to him that all learners are unique and have an individual blend of needs. You could say that inclusion is to special education what child protection is to safeguarding: inclusivity and keeping children safe applies to all learners. However, in some cases, we need to go further to provide more specialist intervention.

The best thing you can do for your students is to become an expert in *them*. Building up a bank of knowledge of the characteristics of neurodiverse conditions, such as autism spectrum disorder (ASD) or ADHD, can help you to support your students. But the bottom line is that when you know one autistic person, you know only that one autistic person. Every profile and every person is different. I know it sounds obvious but it is worth repeating: every one of your students is a unique package of knowledge and skills.

Pause Point

How well do you understand your current students? What is the evidence for this?

....

....

How could you improve on this?

....

....

What systems could you put in place to ensure you get to know as much as you need to about new students in the future?

....

....

Glossary of Terms

Since we don't always know what we don't know, here are some definitions of key terms that you can use as a jumping off point for your own investigations. Please note that whilst the ideas below are based on my own personal, professional and academic experience, they are neither extensive nor complete. Please do your own research for every student who comes to you for support.

Alternative provision (AP). Education provided outside of mainstream schooling for children experiencing difficulties because of mental or physical health issues, permanent exclusion or additional needs. It is usually arranged by local authorities or schools.

Attention deficit hyperactivity disorder (ADHD). A condition that affects behaviour, development or functioning. People with ADHD can seem restless, struggle to concentrate or act impulsively.

Autism spectrum disorder (ASD). People with autism experience and think about the world in different ways from other people. It isn't a disease or an illness but something with which one is born. Autism encompasses a range of conditions, including repetitive behaviours and difficulties with social skills, speech and communication.

Bipolar disorder. Previously known as manic depression, bipolar disorder causes extreme mood swings that include emotional highs (mania or hypomania) and lows (depression).

Depression. Depression is about more than feeling sad or unhappy. It is low mood disorder that can last for weeks, months or even years. Mild depression can affect everyday life and prevent a person from taking interest in other people and activities. More severe depression can lead to suicidal feelings.

Dyscalculia. A learning disability that results in difficulties in understanding numbers and mathematical concepts.

Dyslexia. The British Dyslexia Society defines dyslexia as 'a learning difficulty that primarily affects the skills involved in accurate and fluent word reading and spelling. Characteristic features of dyslexia are difficulties in phonological awareness, verbal memory and verbal processing speed. Dyslexia occurs across the range of intellectual abilities.'[3]

---

3   See https://www.bdadyslexia.org.uk/dyslexia/about-dyslexia/what-is-dyslexia.

Education, health and care (EHC) plan. EHC plans are for children and young people under the age of 25 who need extra support.

Education otherwise than at school (EOTAS). The education or special educational provision for children or young people who are unable to attend a mainstream or special school.

Emotionally based school avoidance (EBSA). Commonly used to describe children and young people who experience difficulties in attending school because of emotional and physical distress. This can lead to an unwillingness to attend and further cycles of anxiety.

Equality, diversity, inclusion, sexuality and gender identity. Being discriminated against, underrepresented and marginalised is a common source of mental health struggles in adults and children. In particular, members of the LGBT+ community are 'at a greater risk of poor mental health and wellbeing' than their peers.[4] According to Stonewall's *LGBT in Britain: Health Report* from 2018:[5]

- 52% of LGBT people said they experienced depression in the previous year.

- 13% of LGBT people between the ages of 18 and 24 said they had attempted to take their own life.

- 14% of LGBT people avoid seeking healthcare for fear of discrimination.

  Play your part in creating an inclusive culture for all your students by being proactive about improving representation and challenging stereotypes. If you're anything like me, and you feel this isn't an area you can address with confidence, start by staying curious and keeping an open mind and an empathetic heart.

4   See https://www.rethink.org/advice-and-information/living-with-mental-illness/information-on-wellbeing-physical-health-bame-lgbtplus-and-studying-and-mental-health/lgbtplus-mental-health/.

5   See https://www.stonewall.org.uk/resources/lgbt-britain-health-2018.

Executive function. A set of skills which 'underlie the capacity to plan ahead and meet goals, display self-control, follow multiple-step directions even when interrupted, and stay focused despite distractions'.[6]

Foetal alcohol spectrum disorder (FASD). A group of permanent conditions that can occur in someone exposed to alcohol before birth. The effects of FASD can include physical problems (e.g. movement, hearing, vision, speech) and problems with behaviour and learning (e.g. managing emotions, social skills, memory, concentration).[7]

Generalised anxiety disorder (GAD). A long-term mental health condition that causes fear, worry and anxiety about a wide range of everyday situations and issues. GAD can cause both psychological and physical symptoms. These vary from person to person but can include feeling restless or worried and having trouble concentrating or sleeping.

Hypermobility spectrum disorder (HSD). These comprise 'connective tissue disorders that cause joint hypermobility, instability, injury, and pain'. HSD can also cause tiredness, headaches and gastrointestinal problems.[8]

Neurodiversity. The word neurodiversity acknowledges the fact that we all experience the world in different ways, so there is no right or wrong way and 'differences are not viewed as deficits'. However, it is often used to describe people with autism, ADHD and other learning disabilities.[9]

Obsessive compulsive disorder (OCD). A mental health disorder where a person has obsessive thoughts or ideas that result in compulsive behaviours. Repetitive activities can include hand washing, cleaning, checking or counting, and can significantly interfere with daily life.

---

6   See https://developingchild.harvard.edu/resources/
    what-is-executive-function-and-how-does-it-relate-to-child-development.
7   See https://www.nhs.uk/conditions/foetal-alcohol-spectrum-disorder.
8   See https://www.ehlers-danlos.com/what-is-hsd.
9   See https://www.health.harvard.edu/blog/what-is-neurodiversity-202111232645.

Occupational therapy (OT). Occupational therapists support people with physical or mental health issues or those whose environment or social circumstances make it challenging for them to participate in important everyday activities.

Pathological demand avoidance (PDA). A pattern of behaviour, often seen in people with autism, to avoid ordinary demands and expectations to an extreme extent, even when it would be of benefit to them.

Sensory processing disorder (SPD). A disorder that affects the way the brain processes multisensory information. SPD can affect all the senses – vision, hearing, smell, taste, touch, vestibular, proprioception and interoception – or just one.

Special educational needs and disabilities (SEND). A child or young person has a special educational need or disability if they have a learning problem and/or a disability which makes it more difficult for them to learn than other children their age.

Special educational needs coordinator (SENCO). The member of staff in a school responsible for assessing, monitoring and coordinating SEND support.

Trauma response. The way we respond to unexpected or distressing events – from major disasters and physical or psychological violence through to personal events, like grief, bullying or divorce – is typified by four mechanisms: fight, flight, freeze or fawn.

Pause Point

What does learning without limits mean to you?

....

....

What specific needs can you identify in your students?

....

....

What adjustments could you make to your tutoring to become more inclusive of students with specific barriers to learning?

....

....

Mental health is the pandemic of our times.

We All Have Mental Health

I used to avoid delivering training on mental health because I felt that I had no right to do so. I felt guilty talking about an area in which I had very limited lived experience. I don't have that problem any more.

Mental health is the pandemic of our times. Indian philosopher Jiddu Krishnamurti said, 'It is no measure of health to be well-adjusted to a profoundly sick society.'[10] I think he might have been right. As I write this, I have a puppy at my feet and a teenage son, Benjamin, to my left. It is ten o'clock on a Thursday morning and my son is supposed to be at school. For the past six months, he has been struggling with anxiety and depression. At the beginning of 2023, Benjamin was unable to attend school due to a crippling fear of everything from a bus crash to a terrorist attack to a zombie apocalypse. He was what the mental health community calls 'in crisis'.

According to the World Health Organization, 'In 2019, 1 in every 8 people, or 970 million people around the world were living with a mental disorder, with anxiety and depressive disorders the most common. In 2020, the number of people living with anxiety and depressive disorders rose significantly because of the COVID-19 pandemic.'[11]

This was the low point for both of us. Benjamin's anxiety triggered my own; I felt his sadness so deeply it hurt. We would attend meetings with the school where they pointed out that 'mum' (i.e. me) was clearly struggling too. How could I not have been? Benjamin and I are very close. We are also very similar; his struggles felt painfully familiar.

Since then, Benjamin has worked with a therapist, and so have I. We were both given antidepressants. My husband and I have been going to relationship counselling. Benjamin exercises regularly. And, most wonderfully of all, we brought Moxie, a gorgeous black

---

10   See https://kfoundation.org/it-is-no-measure-of-health-to-be-well-adjusted-to-a-profoundly-sick-society.
11   World Health Organization, Mental Disorders (8 June 2022). Available at: https://www.who.int/news-room/fact-sheets/detail/mental-disorders.

Labrador puppy into our home. Things are slowly getting better, but there is a long way to go.

Benjamin currently attends school for one hour a day, and most of that is spent in a quiet office with his headphones on. Educational goals have taken a back seat and will have to remain there for a while longer. My next goal is to pursue an ADHD diagnosis for my son. Diagnoses get a bad reputation. People query how useful they are when you can just as easily give the intervention without them. What I have learned is that you only need a label when you need a label. Therefore, if there is a specific benefit, such as support, funding or guidance, that is only available once you have a formal diagnosis, then it is worth taking the time and spending the money to make one happen.

The hardest part of this journey has been the shame. Every time we meet a new professional, I have had to go through the whole story from birth until now. Nothing is left out. Nothing is private. And still I feel judged.

I am sharing my personal story here because I know it can help. Countless tutors have told me that hearing about our journey and progress has helped them with their own. By speaking out, I have discovered that many tutors have their own experiences with neurodiversity and mental health. Of course they do. We are the canaries, the phoenixes and the doves. We have learned gentler ways to live and work. We have learned our strengths and our limitations.

Every situation is unique and every individual has their own journey, but there are some common factors that are useful to consider.

Childhood Development, Attachment and Trauma

As babies, we are wonderfully selfish and self-centred. We take what we need because that is the only way to survive. As we grow up, we become more aware of those around us, of their needs and opinions. We learn that we are dependent on the pleasures of others. We can no longer wail like a baby to have our needs met; instead, we learn to please – or, at least, not to displease.

We all have behaviours that started as a response to our environment and have become habituated. For example, if a baby senses that her mother becomes anxious when she tries to walk, she may be slow to walk. She has learned that her main caregiver, on whom she is entirely dependent, becomes a little less reliable when she steps out on her own, and she understands that it may be safer to stay where she is.

What does this mean for a tutor? Well, for a start, it should illustrate how much is happening below the surface and deep in the past. This suggests that we should try to find out as much about our students as possible to anticipate their needs. It also invites us to keep our minds open to what else may be going on for a child. No matter how well we plan, we can't control all the factors.

A child might not ask questions, not because of anything we are doing wrong, but because the adults who raised her didn't appreciate her curious mind. A parent might respond to your communication with defensiveness, not because you were rude but because they have learned that the world can be a hostile place. As with everything, the better you know yourself, your students and the people around them, the more able you will be to interpret their responses and plan around them.

Fight, Flight, Freeze, Flop or Fawn

Much has been written about this natural physiological trauma response. It seems that we each have one of these behaviours that we switch into automatically in times of heightened anxiety. It has been useful in my own life for me to understand which is my go-to (I freeze or flop) and which are the go-tos of the people around me (they mostly fight).

It can be incredibly helpful to notice this in your students. Consider how they respond when they are under pressure. Do they change the subject (flight) or do they try to please you (fawn)? Do they respond to a difficult question like a rabbit caught in the headlights (freeze) or do they get combative and tell you why theirs is the right answer (fight)?

Knowing that we all display these responses can normalise this behaviour, and in some cases you can even point them out to your student, although possibly not in the moment of stress.

Self-Harm and Suicidal Ideation

According to the mental health charity YoungMinds, in 2018–2019, '24% of 17-year-olds reported having self-harmed in the previous year' and 7% reported having 'self-harmed with suicidal intent at some point in their lives'.[12] The NSPCC explain that 'the physical pain is a distraction from the emotional pain they are struggling with', and list some experiences and emotions that can make children more likely to self-harm. These include:

- Depression, anxiety or eating problems.

- Low self-esteem.

- Bullying and loneliness.

- Emotional, physical or sexual abuse or neglect.

- Grieving or family issues.

- Feeling angry, numb or lacking control.[13]

If you suspect self-harm in your students, you should report it as a safeguarding issue. If you believe that they are in immediate danger or likely to put their life at risk, they should be taken to the closest A&E department, where they will be assessed by the local Child and Adolescent Mental Health Services (CAMHS) team.

. . . .

12 See https://www.youngminds.org.uk/about-us/media-centre/mental-health-statistics.
13 See https://www.nspcc.org.uk/keeping-children-safe/childrens-mental-health/self-harm.

Social Media and Its Antidotes

Social media use may trigger feelings of inadequacy in young people. It may expose them to cyber bullying. It may have adverse effects on sleep. It may increase feelings of isolation.

The research on the association between social media use and the current mental health pandemic is still in its infancy, but the fact that social media use has increased over the same period that mental health has declined is a strong correlation.

Speak with your students about limiting their use of social media and about getting outdoors, or take them outside during your sessions. Encourage exercise – another activity you can bring into your sessions – and, of course, focus on real-life relationship building. Tutoring is a highly relational discipline, and this in itself can enable you to role-model the healthy use of social media and the internet.

Environmental Adjustments

I have been reminded of the importance of environmental adjustments in raising our puppy, Moxie. She tends to get herself into trouble when she is overstimulated. It reminds me of when my own kids were little and I discovered that without sufficient sleep and routine they were impossible to live with. With Moxie, this looks like jumping, biting or toileting in the wrong place. With an overstimulated child, this could look like defiance, disruptiveness or even depression.

What I learned with my own kids, and now with Moxie, is that it is helpful to notice what environmental input you can adapt to change the behaviours. All of these are what our puppy trainer, Charlotte, calls 'control and management' strategies. They are ways to set your student up for success by considering their needs in the way you plan your session. For example, if you are working with a distracted child, consider putting on some instrumental music to help them focus their minds. Find out what they respond to best and use the same playlist each time, so the student associates the music with the desired behaviour.

Consider what else you could do to help your student – perhaps setting a timer for a focused period of working, establishing targets and collecting rewards or using games with a competitive edge. If you are working online and you notice that the sounds of siblings or smells of cooking are distracting them, discuss with the parents whether there is another location or a quieter time that might work better or request a noise-cancelling headset.

Team Around the Child

Even when there are no identified barriers to learning, you should aim to have collegial relationships with the family, the school and other tutors who might be working with the child. Tutoring a student with recognised special educational needs or disabilities might mean that the circle of adults around the child widens. You might be involved with other professionals who are supporting them and their family, such as therapists or social workers.

Effective communication is essential, but it isn't easily achieved. Currently, one preferred way to communicate as a group is WhatsApp, which is quick and unfussy. If this feels overly informal, an email thread can work as a way of documenting progress, and can be useful if you need to maintain a record of interventions. Keep meetings to a minimum and keep them focused. Consider charging for your time to attend meetings. As a freelancer, this is perfectly legitimate since you can't take on any other work during that time.

The most important thing is to establish a high-trust relationship where the various aspects of the child's life can be considered in a holistic way. We must aim to see ourselves as part of the village supporting the child.

Pause Point

What does 'We all have mental health' mean to you?

. . . .

. . . .

What do you consider to be your role in supporting your students' mental health, and where does it end?

. . . .

. . . .

Celebration station

Congratulations! You have just completed all five workshops from the Foundations of Effective Tutoring course. If you email me on julia@qualifiedtutor.com and let me know, I will happily send you a certificate of completion. Who doesn't love a certificate?

Love Tutoring Role Models:
Yuliya Kosko

Yuliya Kosko is a Ukrainian-born tutor living in the UK. When I first met her in 2020, she ran EducAd Consulting, an educational concierge service for international students moving to the UK. But when Russia attacked Ukraine in 2022, she responded by launching a volunteer tutoring service, Svitlo Education, providing a lifeline of support, learning and character development during very dark times.

> *I always wanted to be a teacher, and I always wanted to be surrounded by children. I moved to the UK and did early childhood studies. It coincided with my first child, so it was really cool to have a little boy at home and go through all the theory that I learned at school and university with him.*

Yuliya qualified as a primary school teacher in 2007, specialising in supporting students with English as an additional language:

> *My focus wasn't just on teaching, but teaching international children and making sure they were integrated into whatever new system they entered. But integrated not to the point of losing their identity and culture – learning how to live with both the new culture, the new language, and maintaining their own.*

With the arrival of her second child, the balance tipped between home and work for Yuliya: 'It was too difficult to manage the life and work balance.' That is when she discovered tutoring:

> *International families would get in touch and ask for a consultation or to review their choice of schools. That was the first wave of Russian families coming on investors visas in 2009. I thought I could make a living out of it, and that was a smart decision. I paired up with my friend, who is Slovakian. We*

cofounded EducAd Consulting, which primarily focused on 11+ preparation.

Then it grew into boarding school preparations or applications to boarding schools, mainly for international families. We had these kids who are geniuses in maths, but they struggled with the word questions because of their English.

Then university applications also became very popular because the children that we started with at 11+ grew up and parents were coming back to us asking for help with university applications. Also, our own children have grown up and gone through top universities in the UK, so we thought, 'Oh, we know about it from mum's point of view as well now,' which always helps.

Then everything changed for Yuliya in February 2022 when Russia invaded Ukraine:

I couldn't believe it. Even when there were the satellite images of tanks near Kyiv, I still couldn't believe it. That changed many things in terms of the perspective of what's important in children's well-being, and how good character is probably the main thing that's needed so that it doesn't happen again. As an educator, my immediate reaction was to help Ukrainian children, but at the same time I was thinking about all the Russian children who were now isolated and speaking up against the war and then put in jail at 16.

In March 2022, I got in touch with my teachers who used to teach me in Ukraine, asking if they needed any help and what I could do to help them. I'm not going to go into the sadness of Ukrainian education at the moment, but for many of those children Svitlo is the main source of knowledge, inspiration and motivation. And the teachers that we have volunteering with us, they're idols and mentors and friends.

The Svitlo volunteer tutors support students who are in Ukraine as well as those who are refugees in the UK:

We offer extracurricular lessons in the afternoon. Children can choose which ones they want to join. The main aim is to give something back to Ukrainian children, to teach them English to inspire them and to open up their minds. But I think it's so rewarding for the teachers to see the resilience and the hard work the children put into it, and they also have fun as a teacher creating their own curriculum. Sometimes it's English as an additional language, but sometimes it's pet anatomy or personal finances or investment club or book club. We try to be creative and entertaining. We have a marketing club and a TikTok group.

We focus our attention in the UK on supporting refugee children at GCSE level. When you come as a younger child, it's easier to integrate and learn English, but when you come in Year 10 or Year 11, you have to sit exams and it's very hard. So, our focus is on this under-16 group. Last year, we had a group of Year 11s and we had volunteers for every core subject. The Year 11 group that we had last year all passed their GCSEs and progressed to A levels, and we now have a new group of Year 10 and Year 11. We are hoping to get some funding from the government.

I asked Yuliya how she has the energy to be so productive, and she was refreshingly honest: 'Sometimes I'm just escaping from doing other things. I have my parents living with me, I have two kids, I have the house to look after, so sometimes it's just easier to take a laptop and say, "I'm working – just leave me alone!"' But, of course, the real motivation is the fulfilment tutoring brings:

It's just so rewarding because you are working on this child, and really trying to show all the ways it's possible for them to achieve – and sometimes it's the little decisions that make a huge difference. I think I get my energy from that. I'm a huge believer in online education now because I think it's not in the future; it's here. It's in the present.

What would she say to new tutors just starting out in this profession?

I think the best things happen most of the time when you don't plan for them. Anything you can do, other than sit on the couch and do nothing, will lead to something. So, just don't leave it until tomorrow – go for it. Even if it's going to your local library, starting a small club or volunteering as a story reader – anything.

It's about great opportunities and, of course, people. People make such a huge difference in your life. Career development and tutoring from home can be very lonely. I don't think tutors are competition. I think they are co-workers, partners and colleagues.

Part III

LOVE TUTORING

Chapter 9

CAREER PATHS THROUGH TUTORING

There are many incredible ways to build a viable income through tutoring. Choosing the one that best suits your needs is the work of this chapter, in which we will explore how other tutors operate. As with all businesses, the trick is to find the right model for you.

First, we must get our heads straight on the subject of money. There is nothing wrong with making money from tutoring. Actually, it is necessary. How can you love tutoring if it bankrupts you? The more committed you are to tutoring, the more important it is to ensure that it is financially viable.

Money mindsets hold back many tutors. Yes, talking about money can feel wrong. It can feel misaligned with our values and our wholehearted commitment to helping our students. In our society, there is a tendency to underpay the people who do the most valuable jobs: doctors, nurses, teachers, social workers, carers. We see these vital roles as a calling, a vocation or a way of life rather than as a career. We allow ourselves to believe that fulfilment is its own reward. Tutors love to make a difference, to inspire and change the lives of young people. That is all well and good, but we must remember to change our own lives too.

Setting prices is complex, and tutors who charge more are not necessarily better. At the time of writing, an hourly rate in the UK is between £20 and £80 (£30–£35 is the norm). The good news is that there are plenty of ways to ensure you make enough money without overcharging your clients. Finding the right way for you will depend on where you are in your journey, what your goals are and what suits your natural temperament. As you read through the examples below, try to stay open and curious. You will probably have a knee-jerk preference for one business model over another, but with a little adjustment, any one of these businesses could turn out to be the right approach for you.

Do Your Research

Although tutoring tends to fly under the radar, there is a growing infrastructure on which you can lean. There are professional development communities, including Qualified Tutor, which exist to offer support. There are also groups on social media, usually led by tutor business coaches, which provide information and guidance.

Explore by reading the websites of the tutoring agencies and marketplaces that seem most relevant to you. Just spend some time googling and see what comes up. If you do decide to work with an agency or list your services on a marketplace, take care to choose companies that align with your values and needs. For instance, if you are aiming to serve the private education sector, make sure the agencies you enrol with are positioned to serve those clients.

If you would prefer to stay independent, as I did, you will need to start getting the word out. Think about who you could connect with, such as local schools, social media or your personal community. At some point, you are going to have to put yourself out there, so you may want to start thinking about how this will work. You can pick up lots of tips on this in the various tutoring communities you can connect with online.

Do Your Thinking

Once you have a sense of the possible, spend some time identifying the type of tutoring career that will work for you. It is vital that you own this process. If you are going to have a career in tutoring you love, it needs to be on your terms.

Start by working out why tutoring could be the right route for you. Is it because of the flexible hours? Is it so you can study, work or care for someone at the same time? Is it because you can't stand your current work situation, and, if so, how are you going to ensure that this is different? Try to identify all the drivers for this move, both practical and philosophical, and build them into your plan. For example, if you want to be available for your kids in the evening, you may want to seek international work or find a way to provide tutoring interventions in a local school. If you have an underlying health issue, you may want to specialise in online tutoring. If you are a high energy personality, you may be better suited to group tuition. If you have a doctorate, you may want to offer support to university students in your subject.

The crucial insight here is that tutoring is not only personalised to the student. It is also personalised to the tutor. You can niche down as far as you like; if you become a specialist in your field, there will always be students out there who will want what you have to offer.

Tutoring
is not only
**personalised
to the
student.**
It is also
**personalised
to the tutor.**

Safe, Skilled, Supported Checklist

We've come a long way together now. We've rejected the old views of tutoring and we're looking towards new norms. We've accepted that building independent, confident learners is our ultimate aim. We've begun to find our own unique path to love tutoring.

But none of this new way of thinking will last unless we set ourselves up for success. None of it will be sustainable unless we put the right structures in place. This is where it all comes back to being safe, skilled and supported.

For you to be the tutor your student needs, you need to ensure your own wellbeing. As we now know, even the most competent tutors can feel vulnerable, insecure and lonely. Complete this safe, skilled and supported checklist to explore how ready you are:

Safe

Do you have:

 Police record check at an appropriate level for teachers (in the UK this is called Enhanced DBS on the Update Service)?

 Safeguarding training including all the current information applicable to the teaching profession?

 Insurance policy including professional indemnity and personal liability?

 Terms and conditions?

 Verified client reviews?

Skilled

Do you have:

 Relevant qualifications in the subject matter to the level you are tutoring or above?

 Relevant experience in delivering the subject matter to the level you are tutoring or above?

 Relevant training in how to tutor effectively?

 Additional skills or expertise such as coaching, dyslexia assessment or anything else relevant to serving the needs of your student?

Supported

Do you have:

 Peers and mentors with whom you can talk tutoring?

 Access to relevant business expertise including marketing, invoicing, book keeping, human resources?

 Professional development relevant to your professional learning goals?

 Opportunities to raise standards in the tutoring profession through volunteering, or as a coach or mentor to other tutors?

Celebration station

You know the drill: email me your score for the safe, skilled, supported checklist to julia@qualifiedtutor.com.

Starting and Scaling

You have decided why you want to tutor, and what, how, when and where. Now it is time to find your clients. There are three main routes: signing up to an agency or platform, social media marketing and networking.

Independent tutors find the freedom and flexibility of their role satisfying. They are proactive and thrive on the success of their students. Helen Osmond, the maths tutor from Chapter 2 who left teacher training college for personal reasons, is the epitome of the independent tutor. She has two young children and aims to tutor for sixteen hours per week. After ten years of tutoring, she now has her schedule filled by the start of the academic year, which gives her peace of mind and an immense sense of pride.

One of the challenges for independent tutors is how to increase their earning power. To earn more, they will need to free up more hours, raise their hourly rate, consider group tuition or develop passive income streams.

Freeing up more hours can be tricky, of course. What would you give up to have more time available to tutor? Childcare? Housework? Self-care? If you can do more hours without ruining your work–life balance, it is worth considering.

If you don't want to work longer hours, you may need to charge more. To justify this uplift in prices, think about how you can niche down. As in any profession, there are levels of expertise in tutoring that correspond with the level of specialism and, ultimately, how much they help the student. In other words, a dyslexia assessor can command higher rates than a qualified teacher, who is in turn better paid than an undergraduate tutor. So, consider levelling up your tutoring credibility. You could become a certified children's coach, train to support students with maths anxiety or become a reading recovery specialist. The more you skill up, the more you can charge for your time.

But you don't necessarily need to go back to college to increase your earning power. Instead, you could change your tutoring model from one-to-one to group tuition. There are plenty of benefits of group learning for the students: it can feel less intense, provide valuable peer interaction and bring down the cost of tuition. For the tutor, the main benefit is that you can significantly increase your income.

The hours and way of working will be different from and can complement your tutoring offer. You could create courses for your students or for other tutors, or develop a range of resources that you can sell to others.

If it comes down to supplementing your tutoring income, I have known independent tutors who work in a local café, do some supply teaching or take on virtual assistant work. There is absolutely nothing wrong with having a portfolio career where you do a little bit of a lot of things. This can offer a really rewarding balance as long as you enjoy the work and do everything well.

The next step in the life and development of most independent tutors is to build up a small business. This is a great way to clone yourself, so there are lots of tutors out there representing you and bringing in money to build up your income. Most agencies will take a commission on every hour of tutoring delivered. Taking a cut of other people's work can feel uncomfortable, but if you are the one who takes on the responsibility of finding work for everyone, then that commission is well justified.

Be warned though: as with every business, managing staff, overseeing quality assurance, finding work and compliance will quickly replace the actual tutoring you started out doing. This may feel like a natural progression, and you may enjoy the new challenge, but it is a different career and not suited to everyone.

If you do decide to take on staff, go back to the start of this chapter and go through the entire process again, factoring in the new concept. What type of business do you want to create? How will it work? What infrastructure will it need? What else is out there that is comparable? What type of tutors will you take on? What will make your company special?

Johnny Manning, our boy-next-door archetype from Chapter 2 who started tutoring maths as a sixth former in his local village, built a business based on the success of this experience. He engages undergraduates to teach small-group tuition in schools. Johnny found that the 'near peer' model worked well for high school students, who liked having more relatable role models. He built relationships with the top universities in London and recruits students who have already passed their rigorous entrance requirements. Johnny learned to manage hundreds of boys (and girls)-next-door. He sends them all through our Qualified Tutoring training – in fact, they complete the same five workshops that we cover in Part II of this book. He places a strong emphasis on professionalism, reminding them frequently about safeguarding and professional conduct.

The Manning's model has been replicated frequently since he launched, especially since the NTP funded school-based tuition at scale, but when he started out it was almost unheard of. Don't be afraid to have a left-field idea or invent a new business model for tutoring. If it works, it doesn't matter what has gone before. Tutors are, after all, a profession of innovators and entrepreneurs.

Dogged Determination

Even though you will have designed a career in tutoring you can love, it won't be easy. In fact, that is all the more reason to be sure you love it.

Anne Morris is another tutoring entrepreneur who did things differently. By the time she was a young mum, she had qualified as a maths teacher and as an accountant. She had two previous business start-ups under her belt, and she was ready for the next challenge. Whilst at home one day she caught the daytime news and heard a story about kids leaving school with poor numeracy skills and felt drawn to help.

This was a defining moment for Anne. She had seen these low standards first hand. Having tutored friends' children and seen what a difference she could make simply by slowing maths down and paying more attention to the student, she wondered how she could scale things up. Anne lighted upon the idea of gap-year students, now known as Yipiyaps, which stands for 'Young Inspiring People Inspiring Young Aspiring People'. These school leavers, who had good grades and were typically on their way to university, were placed in schools to tutor students just a few years younger than they were.

She started with two young tutors and one willing head teacher. Twelve years on, there are around one hundred Yipiyaps going into schools each year. Since Yipiyap tutors are themselves young people, Anne and her business partner, Catherine, feel a significant duty of care to ensure that they flourish during their year-long placements. They support their tutors on every level, including continuing professional development, regular check-ins and social events.

When I interviewed Anne for this book, I asked her what word of advice she would give to anyone going on a journey as ambitious as the one she has been on. She didn't mince her words: 'You need dogged determination every step of the way.' She added, 'It's not easy, but if you really believe that what you're doing is the right thing, it's worth it.'

Finally, Find Your Element

It has taken 186 pages to get here, but it is now time. Having covered the basics of tutoring, the options within tutoring and, of course, the misconceptions about tutoring, it is time for you to find your Element as a tutor.

Sir Ken Robinson defined the four aspects of the Element as aptitude, passion, attitude and opportunity – or 'I get it; I love it; I want it; Where is it?'[1] That is to say, to find your Element you need to consider

---

1   K. Robinson and L. Aronica, *The Element: How Finding Your Passion Changes Everything* (New York: Penguin, 2009), p. 22.

your own talents and desires as well as what is happening in your environment.

My process of finding my Element in tutoring was all about reflecting on my leadership style. I loved developing the adults to improve the outcomes for students. I was excited about a community-based and socially minded enterprise. I felt passionate about bringing people together and raising them up.

Meanwhile, Kayleigh Rapson, the early years SENDCO from Part I who opened an alternative provision setting, is all about making life better for neurodiverse children. And Gospel Eadweardfilia, the pharmacist from Part I who got herself out of student debt through tutoring, is all about financial management training for children and families. Yuliya Kosko from Part II, founder of Svitlo Education, which provides volunteer tutoring for Ukrainian students, is all about broadening the horizons of young people living through war.

You might be all about getting more women into science, like Georgina Green, the STEM tutor from Chapter 2. Or you may be passionate about improving the level of numeracy in the next generation of British children, like Anne Morris from Yipiyap, who we met earlier in this chapter. You might be most excited about bringing a comprehensive education to neurodiverse students online, like Kirstin Coughtrie of Gaia Learning in Chapter 2. Or you may be determined to make the 11+ less traumatic, like Anita Oberoi, the test prep tutor from Chapter 2.

It may be any of these things, or reading recovery, academic coaching or careers advice. It may be entrepreneurialism, edtech or AI. The options are vast.

This is your opportunity to dig deep and consider what your aptitude (I get it), your passion (I love it), your attitude (I want it) and your opportunity (Where is it?) point towards. Hopefully the questions in this pause point will help.

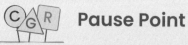
🚏 Pause Point

Aptitude (I get it)

Think about a time in your life when time flew. What were you focused on?

....

....

Think about a time in your life when you felt really confident. What were you doing?

....

....

Think about what people compliment you on. What are the common themes?

....

....

Passion (I love it)

Think about what topics you enjoy reading about or discussing. What are your areas of special interest?

....

....

Think about who you most enjoy working with. Is it adults or children? Special educational needs students or academic high-flyers?

. . . .

. . . .

Think about a time in your career when you have felt stretched and stimulated. What was it about that role that excited you?

. . . .

. . . .

Attitude (I want it)

Consider who you were as a child. What did you love doing back then that you could still love now, if it weren't for all that limited thinking?

. . . .

. . . .

Opportunity (Where is it?)

What could a role look like that combined all the ideas in your answers above?

. . . .

. . . .

What is becoming clear about your patterns and preferences?

. . . .

. . . .

What areas might you want to research further?

....

....

If you found your Element in tutoring, how would it feel?

....

....

Celebration station

This is the big one. Please email me and let me know what you think your Element might be. It doesn't need to be a complete picture just yet, but if you are beginning to get an inkling for how you might fly in tutoring, you know I want to know about it! Email me at julia@qualifiedtutor.com.

Chapter 10

UP AND OUT

It has been a while now since I was a lonely young tutor, frustrated by classroom teaching, impossible childcare costs and my own professional insecurity. In fact, I miss those early days when life was simple and I knew what and where I needed to be. In recent years, the dream has grown up. It is now, like the rest of my kids, an impossible teenager: demanding, unpredictable, irrepressibly idealistic. It won't be satisfied until it has saved the world – or, at least, until tutoring gets the love it deserves.

Love Tutoring is not just a soppy notion or marketing spiel. It is a question, an invitation and a provocation. It also has some of the most robust evidence in education behind it. Professor John Hattie, whose meta-analysis we looked at in Chapter 7, shows that 'collective teacher efficacy', defined as 'the collective belief of teachers in their ability to positively affect students',[1] is the most powerful determiner of outcomes for students. Of course, this collective belief must be based on more than mere positive thinking. It must be developed through ongoing professional dialogue and the development of shared beliefs and practices. Collective efficacy is a 'collaborative conversation based on evidence';[2] in other words, when we learn together what does work, what doesn't work and why, we can learn to believe in ourselves and each other. As always, we

---

1   See https://visible-learning.org/2018/03/collective-teacher-efficacy-hattie.
2   S. J. Langford, An Examination of Professional Support in the Life of the Experienced Urban Primary Teacher (PhD dissertation, University of Plymouth, 2020), p. 108. Available at: https://pearl.plymouth.ac.uk/bitstream/handle/10026.1/16137/2020LANGFORD10600725PhD.pdf.

are talking about improving outcomes for students by developing the adults who work with them.

If this is important for teaching, how much more so for tutoring? Those of us who work outside of school, out of hours and without colleagues have much to gain from this evidence. If we are this effective alone, imagine how powerful we can be together.

To undertake this learning and amplify our success, we need to bring together independent tutors to become something more than a disparate collection of freelancers. This is the 'Big Hairy Audacious Goal'[3] of Qualified Tutor.

Be Like Bamboo

I am no ecologist, but in my imagination school might be represented by an oak tree, whilst tutoring is more like bamboo. We need oak trees. We need them to create structure and stability in the landscape. We need them to give shelter and habitats to many living communities. But we also need bamboo, a versatile and diverse group of plants that are hardy and fast-growing. What I find helpful about this metaphor is the implication of the power of tutoring in the wider ecosystem. Bamboo is not only sustainable and adaptable, but it is also regenerative and restorative to the soil in which it grows. As I learned from the Global Landscapes Forum: 'Bamboo can be a powerful ally for land restoration. This strategic resource thrives on problem soils and steep slopes, helps to conserve soil and water, and improves land quality.'[4] Tutoring rehabilitates teaching and learning, just as bamboo rehabilitates the environment, making it a powerful ally in education reform.

- -

3   J. Collins, *Good to Great: Why Some Companies Make the Leap … and Others Don't* (New York: HarperCollins, 2001), p. 190.
4   See https://archive.globallandscapesforum.org/bamboo-a-powerful-ally-for-land-restoration.

Tutoring **rehabilitates** teaching and learning, making it a **powerful ally** in **education reform**.

What I Know for Sure

Inspired by Oprah Winfrey's wonderful book *What I Know for Sure,* here are some of the truths I have learned about tutoring:

- It is time to stop waiting for permission and start creating the change in education that really needs to happen.

- The greatest strength of tutoring is how complex and diverse it is. This is also its greatest weakness.

- To love tutoring, you need to be safe, skilled and supported. Tutoring in a silo will rarely be successful or sustainable.

- Tutoring is an agile and open space, ideally suited to entrepreneurs and idealists. It is not suited to cowboys or hustlers.

- There is more than one way to be an educator, and the sooner we realise this, the happier we will be.

- A more fluid approach to teaching and tutoring could make employment in education a more attractive option.

Just Imagine

Imagine a school timetable in which tutors and teachers work side by side, leaning into their strengths. The teacher would run a bustling classroom where students would support and challenge each other in open-ended activities. The tutor would focus on functional skills, working with every student in rotation on an individualised learning pathway, ensuring that, really and truly, no student is left behind.

Imagine a teaching career where tutoring is a legitimate branch on the pathway. Imagine the depth of subject knowledge that tutors would develop. Imagine the improvements they could achieve in their practice by focusing on the teaching and learning without the distractions of classroom management. Imagine how safe the teacher would feel going to their school leader and asking for a secondment to the tutoring staff, so they could recharge their batteries before burning out.

Imagine a future where an agile, adaptable curriculum is delivered by adaptive computer-based learning, and each student is nurtured by a caring, committed lead learner who feels like a safe, trusted adult.

Imagine an education sector with tutors and teachers working together as mutually respected experts. Imagine a whole department of one-to-one rooms with open doors, willing tutors and zero stigma. Imagine a school where everyone knew that the needs of every child would be met. Imagine the joined-up planning there could be between tutors and teachers, with tutors contributing to teacher-assessed examinations, to school reports and education, to EHC plans. Imagine the professional dialogue. Imagine the quality of support the student would receive.

Imagine a society of people who haven't spent their childhoods competing in an impossible race. Imagine a society of people who are set up for success.

Now imagine your role within that future. Imagine yourself as a contributor to a new way of teaching and learning. Imagine yourself as a leader, pointing towards gentler ways to improve outcomes. Imagine yourself as the dove, flying off to find dry land. Just imagine.

REFERENCES

Anderson, L. W. and Krathwohl, D. R. (eds) (2001). *A Taxonomy for Learning, Teaching, and Assessing: A Revision of Bloom's Taxonomy of Educational Objectives* (New York: Longman).

Bartlett, S. (2023). *The Diary of a CEO: The 33 Laws of Business and Life* (London: Ebury Edge).

Bettinger, D. (2018). Life 2.0 Innate Health Conference, London, 13–15 May.

Bloom, B. S. (ed.) (1956). *Taxonomy of Educational Objectives: The Classification of Educational Goals. Handbook I: Cognitive Domain* (New York: David McKay Company).

Brown, P. and Levinson, S. (1978). Universals in Language Usage: Politeness Phenomena. In E. N. Goody (ed.), *Questions and Politeness* (Cambridge: Cambridge University Press), pp. 56–289.

Burtonshaw, S. and Simons, J. (2023). *The Future of Tutoring* (London: Public First). Available at: https://www.impetus.org.uk/assets/publications/The-Future-of-Tutoring.pdf.

Collins, J. (2001). *Good to Great: Why Some Companies Make the Leap … and Others Don't* (New York: HarperCollins).

Cullinane, C. and Montacute, R. (2023). *Tutoring – The New Landscape: Recent Trends in Private and School-Based Tutoring* (London: Sutton Trust). Available at: https://www.suttontrust.com/our-research/tutoring-2023-the-new-landscape.

Department for Education (2023). *Keeping Children Safe in Education 2023: Statutory Guidance for Schools and Colleges. Part One: Information for All School and College Staff* (1 September). Available at: https://www.gov.uk/government/publications/keeping-children-safe-in-education--2.

Fazackerley, A. (2023). Revealed: Stress of Ofsted Inspections Cited as Factor in Deaths of 10 Teachers, *The Observer* (25 March). Available at: https://www.theguardian.com/education/2023/mar/25/revealed-stress-of-ofsted-inspections-cited-as-factor-in-deaths-of-10-teachers.

Ginott, H. G. (1972). *Teacher and Child: A Book for Parents and Teachers* (New York: Macmillan).

Gladwell, M. (2008). *Outliers: The Story of Success* (New York: Little, Brown & Co.).

Godin, S. (2008). *Tribes: We Need You to Lead Us*. London: Piatkus.

Godin, S. (2023). *The Song of Significance: A New Manifesto for Teams* (London: Penguin Business).

Hattie, J. (1992). Measuring the Effects of Schooling. *Australian Journal of Education*, 36(1), 5–13. Available at: https://www.nzcer.org.nz/nzcerpress/set/articles/measuring-effects-schooling.

Hattie, J. (2009). *Visible Learning: A Synthesis of Over 800 Meta-Analyses Relating to Achievement* (New York: Routledge).

Hopf, G. M. (2016). *Those Who Remain: A Postapocalyptic Novel*, Vol. 7 (New World Series) (N.p.: CreateSpace).

Jackson, W. P. (1990). *Life in Classrooms* (New York: Teachers College Press).

Jones, J. (2011). *The Magic-Weaving Business: Finding the Heart of Learning and Teaching* (Stradbally, Co. Waterford: Leannta Publishing).

Kahneman, D. (2012). *Thinking, Fast and Slow* (London: Allen Lane).

Karpicke, J. D. (2016). A Powerful Way to Improve Learning and Memory. *Psychological Science Agenda*, 30(6).

Lampl, P. (2016). Foreword. In P. Kirby, *Shadow Schooling: Private Tuition and Social Mobility in the UK* (London: Sutton Trust), p. 1. Available at: https://www.suttontrust.com/our-research/shadowschooling-private-tuition-social-mobility.

Langford, S. J. (2020). An Examination of Professional Support in the Life of the Experienced Urban Primary Teacher (PhD dissertation, University of Plymouth). Available at: https://pure.plymouth.ac.uk/ws/portalfiles/portal/38477993/2020LANGFORD10600725PhD.pdf.

Major, L. E., Tyers, E. and Chu, R. (2020). The National Tutoring Service: Levelling-Up Education's Playing Field. Available at: https://www.exeter.ac.uk/media/universityofexeter/collegeofsocialsciencesandinternationalstudies/education/documentsfordownload/National_Tutoring_Service_April_2020.pdf.

Martin, M. (2023). Teachers Leaving at Highest Rate in Four Years, *TES* (8 June). Available at: https://www.tes.com/magazine/news/general/retention-crisis-teachers-leaving-highest-rate-years.

Milken Institute School of Public Health (2020). Equity vs. Equality: What's the Difference? *George Washington University* (5 November). Available at: https://onlinepublichealth.gwu.edu/resources/equity-vs-equality/.

Morrison McGill, R. (2017). *Mark. Plan. Teach.* (London: Bloomsbury Education).

Myatt, M. (2016). *High Challenge, Low Threat: How the Best Leaders Find the Balance* (Woodbridge: John Catt Educational).

Myatt, M. (2023). Intellectual Architecture [blog] (22 June). Available at: https://www.marymyatt.com/blog/intellectual-architecture.

National Society for the Prevention of Cruelty to Children (2021a). *Statistics Briefing: Child Sexual Abuse* (March). Available at: https://learning.nspcc. org.uk/media/1710/statistics-briefing-child-sexual-abuse.pdf.

National Society for the Prevention of Cruelty to Children (2021b). *Statistics Briefing: Emotional Abuse* (December). Available at: https://learning.nspcc. org.uk/media/2717/statistics-briefing-emotional-abuse.pdf.

National Society for the Prevention of Cruelty to Children (2021c). *Statistics Briefing: Neglect* (July). Available at: https://learning.nspcc.org.uk/ media/2621/statistics-briefing-neglect.pdf.

National Society for the Prevention of Cruelty to Children (2021d). *Statistics Briefing: Physical Abuse* (September). Available at: https://learning.nspcc. org.uk/media/2669/statistics-briefing-physical-abuse.pdf.

Peacock, A. (2016). Learning Without Limits, *TEDxNorwichED* [video] (28 March). Available at: https://www.youtube.com/watch?v=8oxxPi6c-Nw.

Quinn, P. D. and Duckworth, A. L. (2007). Happiness and Academic Achievement: Evidence for Reciprocal Causality. Paper presented at the Annual Meeting of the American Psychological Society, Washington, DC, 24–27 May.

Rath, T. and Clifton, D. O. (2004). *How Full Is Your Bucket? Positive Strategies for Work and Life* (New York: Gallup Press).

Robinson, K. with Aronica, L. (2009). *The Element: How Finding Your Passion Changes Everything* (New York: Penguin).

Robinson, V. (2017). *Capabilities Required for Leading Improvement: Challenges for Researchers and Developers* [paper presentation]. Research Conference 2017: Leadership for Improving Learning – Insights from Research (Camberwell, VIC: Australian Council for Educational Research), pp. 1–5. Available at: https://research.acer.edu.au/ research_conference/RC2017/28august/2.

Rowe, M. B. (1986). Wait Time: Slowing Down May Be a Way of Speeding Up! *Journal of Teacher Education*, 37(1), 43–50.

Syed, M. (2011). *Bounce: The Myth of Talent and the Power of Practice* (London: Fourth Estate).

Sinek, S. (2009). How Great Leaders Inspire Action, *TED.com* [video] (September). Available at: https://www.ted.com/talks/simon_sinek_ how_great_leaders_inspire_action.

Sinek, S. with Mead, D. and Docker, P. (2017). *Find Your Why: A Practical Guide for Discovering Purpose for You and Your Team* (New York: Portfolio/ Penguin).

Vygotsky, L. S. (1978). *Mind in Society: The Development of Higher Psychological Processes* (Cambridge, MA: Harvard University Press).

White, S., Groom-Thomas, L. and Loeb, S. (2022). *Undertaking Complex But Effective Instructional Supports for Students: A Systematic Review of Research on High-Impact Tutoring Planning and Implementation.* EdWorkingPaper 22-652. Available at: https://files.eric.ed.gov/fulltext/ED625876.pdf.

World Health Organization (2022). Mental Disorders (8 June). Available at: https://www.who.int/news-room/fact-sheets/detail/mental-disorders.

ABOUT THE AUTHOR

Julia Silver lives in North London with her husband, five children and black labrador named Moxie. She is passionate about developing a gentler approach to education that is kinder to everyone involved. This is where her love for tutoring stems.

Julia gained her bachelors degree in English and philosophy at the University of Leeds, her postgraduate certificate in primary education (PGCE) from the University of Lancaster and her national professional qualification in headship (NPQH) from UCL's Institute of Education.

In 2020, Julia founded Qualified Tutor, the professional development organisation for the tutoring profession. Her flagship course, Foundations of Effective Tutoring, which is featured in this book, has now been completed by thousands of tutors worldwide. Since then, Julia created the Love Tutoring Festivals and World Tutors' Day (2nd July) – a series of inclusive, innovative events for tutors.

Today, Qualified Tutor is known for raising standards in tutoring, through membership and certification, events and community, and training and qualifications. We aim to improve outcomes for students by ensuring that the tutors they work with are safe, skilled and supported.

If you enjoyed this book and would like to get more involved, go to www.lovetutoring.com to access special opportunities exclusively for our readers.

The Philosophy Foundation: The Philosophy Shop

Ideas, activities and questions to get people, young and old, thinking philosophically

Peter Worley

ISBN: 978-178135264-9

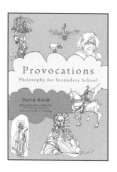

The Philosophy Foundation: Provocations

Philosophy for secondary school

David Birch

ISBN: 978-178583368-7

The Philosophy Foundation: Thoughtings

Puzzles, problems and paradoxes in poetry to think with

Peter Worley and Andrew Day

ISBN: 978-178135087-4

The Philosophy Foundation: The Numberverse

How numbers are bursting out of everything and just want to have fun

Andrew Day

ISBN: 978-184590889-8

Independent Thinking on Teaching and Learning

Developing independence and resilience in all teachers and learners

Jackie Beere

ISBN: 978-178135339-4

In this all-encompassing book on teaching and learning, Independent Thinking Associate Jackie Beere draws on her many years' experience as a teaching assistant, primary teacher and secondary head teacher to re-energise every teacher's passion for their profession.

She champions both children and teachers as learners, and, together with expert advice on how to instill the habits of independent learning in all pupils, shares great practice that delivers outstanding outcomes for all educators.

Jackie encourages teachers to embrace challenge and change, and suggests ways in which they can provide a model for their pupils when it comes to developing independence and resilience. She also offers expert guidance on how teachers can build rapport with their students and cultivate with them a sense of co-ownership of their learning journey so that they work hard, value their learning and fulfil their potential.

Essential reading for all teachers and school leaders who wish to make an impact on the teaching and learning in their school.

www.crownhouse.co.uk

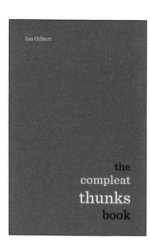

The Compleat Thunks® Book

Ian Gilbert

ISBN: 978-178135272-4

We are living in an age in which facts don't count, certainty no longer exists and complexity means we never quite know what just happened, let alone what will happen next. To better prepare ourselves for such a world, we need a brain workout that isn't so much about finding answers as getting our heads around questions.

We need *The Compleat Thunks Book*, a collection of beguiling questions about everyday things that stop you in your tracks and help you start to look at the world in a whole new light. At times controversial and often provocative, Ian Gilbert's brainteasers are sure to stimulate philosophical enquiry and debate during the thinking, reasoning, logic or panic employed in arriving at (or deviating from) the answers and conversations that ensue. In other words, it's not about the answers at all and, as in life, there are none at the back of the book.

Covering as wide a variation of topics as possible – from love and lies to parking a car and molesting robots – this book will appeal to people of all ages, tastes and prejudices, and can be used to steer pub, dinner party or family discussions away from the same old topics.

Parental Advisory: A few of these Thunks are unsuitable for use with children.

www.crownhouse.co.uk

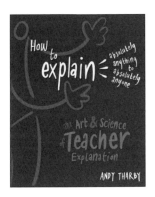

How to Explain Absolutely Anything to Absolutely Anyone

The art and science of teacher explanation

Andy Tharby

ISBN: 978-178583367-0

In *How to Explain Absolutely Anything to Absolutely Anyone*, Andy Tharby eloquently explores the art and science of this undervalued skill and illustrates how improving the quality of explanation can improve the quality of learning. Delving into the wonder of metaphor, the brilliance of repetition and the timeless benefits of storytelling, Andy sets out an evidence-informed approach that will enable teachers to explain tricky concepts so well that their students will not only understand them perfectly, but remember them forever too.

By bringing together evidence and ideas from a wide range of sources – including cognitive science, educational research and the study of linguistics – the book examines how the most effective writers and speakers manage to transform even the most messy, complicated idea into a thing of wondrous, crystalline clarity. Then, by provoking greater thought and contemplation around language choices in the classroom, Andy spells out how the practical tools and techniques discussed can be put into practice.

Brimming with sensible advice applicable to a range of settings and subjects, this book is suitable for teachers and educators of learners aged 7–16.

Powerful Questioning

Strategies for improving learning and retention in the classroom

Michael Chiles

ISBN: 978-178583596-4

Foreword by John Hattie.

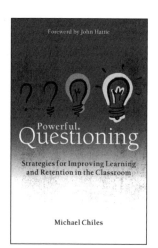

Powerful Questioning: Strategies for improving learning and retention in the classroom by Michael Chiles is an evidence-based examination of the power of questioning in the classroom and how it can be improved.

Questioning is a staple feature of a teacher's toolkit across all phases of education. Classrooms are awash with explanation, modelling and feedback, but of all the pedagogical strategies at a teacher's disposal, questioning is one of the most important. It is the heartbeat of a classroom. While the art of asking a question seems relatively straightforward, to what extent do teachers consider the types of questions they're using? Are the questions they ask students actually helping to support learning? In *Powerful Questioning*, Michael Chiles delves into the complexity of asking questions and how best to use this pedagogical tool as a powerful springboard to support learning in the classroom.

Essential reading for all teachers and school leaders.